(l

by Rob Gibson

Illustrations by Andrew Simpson

© Robert Gibson
First Published 2009
Reprinted September 2011,
October 2012, October 2013.
Updated March 2015, March 2016.
Reprinted April 2017.
The Royal Yachting Association
RYA House, Ensign Way, Hamble,
Southampton SO31 4YA
Tel: 02380 604 100
E-mail: publications@rya.org.uk
Web: www.rya.org.uk
Follow us on Twitter @RYAPublications
or on YouTube
ISBN: 978-1-906435-16-5
RYA Order Code: G81

Note: While all reasonable care had been taken in the preparation
of this book, the publisher takes no responsibility for the use of the
methods or products or contracts described in the book.

Technical Editor: Paul Mara

Cover Design: Batt Creative

Cover photographs: Sunseeker; Northshore

Photo credit: Paul Goldsack

Typesetting and Design: Kevin Slater

Proofreading and indexing: Alan Thatcher

Printed in China through World Print

Totally Chlorine   Sustainable
Free   Forests

FOREWORD

In mainland Europe there is a certain type of official, usually with epaulettes, who will not let you pass in your boat unless you produce an International Certificate of Competence. For these retentive jobsworths even an RYA Yachtmaster certificate is unacceptable; the ICC with its European wording and translations is the only certificate he recognises.

I always take my ICC when yachting in Europe even on coastlines where it is not strictly necessary. On inland waters it is definitely necessary and confirms the holder has passed a test on the Inland Waterways CEVNI regulations.

In 1998 when the UNECE Resolution 40 introduced the ICC, I was given the job of turning a fairly vague syllabus into an RYA assessment, and implementing it at over a thousand RYA recognised practical training centres. The assessment had to be accessible and achievable, but sufficiently rigorous to ensure that holders of the ICC can keep themselves out of trouble.

How this now works and how to obtain an ICC is explained in this book. If you are considering a trip to mainland Europe and need a certificate this book is a must. The syllabus and standard is explained in detail along with a wealth of helpful hints and information on everything from the CEVNI rules to boat handling and collision avoidance.

Rob Gibson, the author, is one of our most experienced instructors and examiners. When he took his RYA Yachtmaster Instructor course his examiner described him as "an excellent instructor and boat handler and a pleasure to be with". You couldn't ask for a better tutor.

James Stevens FRIN

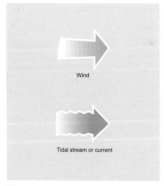

Key to symbols used in illustrations throughout the book

NOTE: The charts and tidal information in this book are taken from RYA Training Charts and RYA Training Manual and are not to be used for navigation

CONTENTS

■ EVIDENCE OF COMPETENCE ABROAD

Many European countries require the skipper of a pleasure craft to be able to provide evidence of his or her competence. Experiences differ greatly. Inconsistency from province to province and port to port means many boaters are never asked to provide evidence of their competence abroad. However, those that are asked and do not have a suitable document can find themselves in an uncomfortable situation. This is where an ICC can prove to be useful.

■ WHAT IS THE ICC?

The ICC (or to give it its full title International Certificate for Operators of Pleasure Craft) is a certificate which is intended to provide evidence of competence when requested by officials in foreign countries. It is sometimes known as the International Certificate of Competence.

It is issued under the United Nations Economic Commission for Europe (UNECE) Inland Transport Committee Working Party on Inland Water Transport Resolution 40. It is this resolution which details how and to whom the ICC may be issued, the syllabus requirements, the layout of the certificate and it also lists the countries which have notified the UNECE Secretariat that they have accepted the resolution.

What does the ICC do?

When you visit another country, in most circumstances (in accordance with the United Nations Convention on the Law of the Sea) you can be required to comply with the maritime legislation of the visited country (the Coastal State) in addition to that of your vessel's country of registration (Flag State).

The regulations for pleasure craft can vary considerably from one country to another and the regime for skipper training and licensing can be equally disparate; the ICC helps to overcome the difficulties these differences can cause.

An ICC issued by a contracting Government to Resolution 40 indicates that the certificate holder has demonstrated the level of competence required by Resolution 40 for the certificate to be issued. In other words it is an assurance from one Government to another that the certificate holder is sufficiently competent to be driving a pleasure craft, despite not holding the visited country's national certificate.

Formal Acceptance of the ICC

The ICC should be automatically accepted in countries which have adopted Resolution 40. However, of the 56 UNECE countries able to accept the resolution, the UK is one of only a handful which have fully adopted Resolution 40. Many of the eligible countries have not accepted Resolution 40, some still apply Resolution 14 which Resolution 40 was intended to replace and others only apply Resolution 40 in part or with caveats attached.

Wider (Informal) Acceptance

The ICC is however a far more useful document than the Resolution's formal acceptance would suggest. Although acceptance of the ICC by the visited country should be because the visited country itself has adopted Resolution 40, the ICC is sometimes recognised as an acceptable certificate in the visited country's national legislation and is quite often accepted on a purely informal basis. Spain, Greece and Portugal, for example, have not adopted Resolution 40 but are still likely to ask visitors for an ICC.

The ICC may be acceptable for visiting foreign flagged vessels, foreign flagged vessels being kept in the Coastal State and / or vessels flagged in the Coastal State. It should never be assumed that the ICC will be accepted as an alternative to the national qualification of the vessel's flag state. The onus is on ICC holders to determine its acceptability by foreign states, as the ICC was never intended to be an alternative to individual national qualification requirements.

Further information about where the RYA recommends having an ICC can be found at www.rya.org.uk/go/icc-accept.

■ WHO CAN GET AN ICC FROM THE RYA?

The RYA is authorised by the Maritime and Coastguard Agency (MCA) to issue the ICC, on behalf of the UK Government, to qualifying individuals. Applicants for a UK ICC issued by the RYA must be eligible to be issued the certificate and must demonstrate the necessary knowledge and skills.

Eligibility

The certificate is available to a person who fulfils the following eligibility criteria:
■ has reached the age of 16
■ is physically and mentally fit to operate a pleasure craft, and in particular, has sufficient powers of vision and hearing
■ presents one of the specified UK certificates or has successfully passed an examination to prove the necessary competence for pleasure craft operation
■ who demonstrates their nationality or residency to show that their nationality does not preclude them from being issued with an ICC by the RYA

Evidence of Nationality or Residency

The RYA is authorised by the Maritime and Coastguard Agency (MCA) to issue a UK ICC to the nationals of any country EXCEPT individuals who are a national of another UNECE member state which has accepted Resolution 40 and who are also resident in another UNECE member state which has accepted Resolution 40, unless the RYA has been given written permission to do so by the Government of the relevant country.

The list of UNECE member states that have accepted Resolution 40 is subject to change without notice (i.e. whenever the government of a country adopts Resolution 40). The current list is available on the RYA website at www.rya.org.uk/go/icc-no.

A person's eligibility can therefore change during the period the ICC is valid for. Should this be the case, the certificate holder must notify the RYA and surrender the certificate; no refunds of any nature will be given. If the certificate holder cannot satisfactorily demonstrate his or her continued eligibility when the certificate expires it will not be renewed by the RYA.

Applicants are required to provide evidence of their eligibility when they first apply for an ICC and must provide evidence that they remain eligible to be issued with the ICC on renewal.

An individual who is not eligible to be issued with an ICC by the RYA (by virtue of their nationality and place of residence) should be able to obtain an ICC from their own Government. They must however note that possession of an RYA certificate does not entitle them to a certificate issued by any other organisation or on behalf of any other national Government.

Individuals with dual nationality may apply for the UK ICC issued by the RYA if either nationality makes them eligible to do so. It should however be noted that only the nationality which made the individual eligible for the certificate to be issued will be recorded on the ICC.

■ DEMONSTRATING THE NECESSARY KNOWLEDGE AND SKILLS

Resolution 40 requires that applicants for the ICC prove that they have sufficient knowledge and ability to safely operate a pleasure craft. This can be done by presenting a recognised national certificate issued by the country which is issuing the ICC. Alternatively the Resolution makes provision for boater to pass an examination.

The UK ICC issued by the RYA has five categories. When an ICC is issued, only the categories for which competence has been demonstrated will be validated. The categories are split into two lists:

List 1: Coastal waters
        Inland waters

List 2: Power
        Sail (including auxiliary engine)
        Personal watercraft

At least one category in each list must be validated.

■ VALIDATING THE COASTAL AND INLAND CATEGORIES

The ICC does not distinguish between tidal and non-tidal coastal waters and Resolution 40 does not set out a comprehensive definition of what is meant by "coastal" and "inland" but the intention is that they are mutually exclusive – i.e. "coastal" is anything that is not "inland".

Resolution 40 does however require that candidates for coastal waters have knowledge of the International Regulations for Preventing Collisions at Sea (COLREGs) and candidates for inland waters have knowledge of the European inland waterways regulations, the Code Européen des Voies de Navigation Intérieure (CEVNI) (See Part B).

Where the applicant took their course or examination normally determines (but with a couple of exceptions) whether or not the coastal waters category will be validated as the syllabus for an eligible RYA or MCA practical course taken on coastal waters includes the COLREGs.

Taking an eligible RYA or MCA practical course does not automatically validate the inland category in the same way. This is because CEVNI is not covered in the UK's courses, as these regulations are not in use in the UK. Every candidate wishing to have the inland category validated on their ICC must therefore first pass the ICC CEVNI test.

Applicants who only have an eligible RYA or MCA practical course completion certificate or certificate of competence taken inland or who take an inland ICC assessment, must pass the CEVNI test to receive an ICC as the certificate would otherwise be invalid.

■ THE ICC CEVNI TEST

You can arrange to take the ICC CEVNI Test through RYA recognised training centres and affiliated clubs that are authorised to carry out the test.

The RYA ICC CEVNI test is a multiple choice paper. Costs for the CEVNI test will vary between organisations (RYA recognised training centres and RYA affiliated clubs).

There are two options:
• Take the test in person at an RYA recognised training centre or an affiliated club authorised to carry out the test; or
• Many RYA recognised training centres or affiliated clubs authorised to carry out the test can provide you with access to take the test online remotely from home or anywhere in the world.

The "RYA European Waterways Regulations (The CEVNI Rules Explained)" publication (G17) provides the information you need to learn the code in a clear and concise way – a sample paper can be found at the back of the book.

In addition to the passing the CEVNI test, for an ICC to be issued you must present a qualifying RYA practical course completion certificate or pass an ICC assessment at an RYA recognised training centre and be eligible to be issued with an ICC.

To find out more about the ICC CEVNI test, please visit:
http://www.rya.org.uk/infoadvice/boatingabroad/icc/Pages/cevnitest.aspx
For further information on the ICC, please visit:
http://www.rya.org.uk/infoadvice/boatingabroad/icc/Pages/ICC.aspx
The CEVNI test is covered in section B of the book.

Validating the type of Vessel Categories

To validate all the categories on an ICC, you will need to be assessed on or present an eligible RYA or MCA practical course completion certificate or certificate of competence to cover each category. It is perfectly acceptable to be assessed for one category and present a certificate for another category.

A table which indicates the eligible courses and the categories they will validate on the ICC is published on the RYA website at www.rya.org.uk/go/icc-evidence.

■ THE ICC ASSESSMENT

Applicants for the UK ICC issued by the RYA who have not yet successfully completed an acceptable RYA or MCA practical course, but already have the required level of competence can take the ICC Assessment to prove their competence.
N.B. The ICC assessment is not applicable to Personal Watercraft.

Arranging to take the Assessment

The ICC assessment can be arranged through an RYA recognised training centre or an affiliated club authorised to carry out the assessment known as an ICC test centre. A convenient ICC test centre can be identified using the 'Where's my Nearest' search on the RYA website. The training centre or club will, confirm your successful completion of the assessment by signing the relevant section of the ICC application form – there is no separate certificate.

Send your signed application form together with the other items required for your application or renewal to the RYA Certification Department.

The Assessment Syllabus

The syllabus for the ICC assessment is detailed on the ICC application form. It comprises oral/written elements and also requires you to demonstrate your skills on the water.

It is reproduced on the following three pages.

SYLLABUS FOR ICC ASSESSMENT OF COMPETENCE

ORAL/WRITTEN ELEMENTS

ALL CANDIDATES

Regulations

1. Knows responsibility for keeping a proper lookout
2. Can determine a 'safe speed'
3. Can recognise a potential collision situation
4. Can identify 'give way' vessel in a collision situation
5. Knows what action to take as 'give way' and 'stand on' vessel
6. Knows responsibilities of small boat in a narrow channel
7. Can recognise manoeuvring signals (1, 2, 3 & 5 short blasts)
8. Can make and recognise visual distress signals

Safety

1. Is able to use and instruct crew in the use of:
   - Lifejackets
   - Distress alerting (e.g. DSC VHF, EPIRB, flares etc.)
   - Fire extinguishers
   - Kill cord (if fitted)

2. Can prepare a boat for use and take sensible precautions before setting out including:
   - Engine checks
   - Check fuel for range/duration of trip
   - Obtain weather forecast
   - Avoid overloading boat

These aspects of the syllabus are discussed in section A of the book.

Regulations

1. Knows the rules relating to traffic separation schemes

2. Knows requirements for navigation lights and shapes to be displayed by own vessel

3. Can recognise the following from the lights: power driven, sailing vessel, vessel at anchor, tug and tow, fishing vessel, dredger

4. Knows sound signals to be made in reduced visibility by vessels in question 3

Navigation

(Chart and plotting instruments required)

1. Can interpret a navigational chart, understand the significance of charted depths and drying heights and can identify charted hazards

2. Can plot position by cross bearings and by latitude/longitude

3. Can determine a magnetic course to steer, making allowances for leeway and tidal stream

4. Can use a tide table to find the times and heights of high and low water at a standard port

5. Can determine the direction and rate of a tidal stream from a tidal stream atlas or tidal diamonds on a chart

6. Understands the basic use of a GPS

Pilotage

1. Can recognise by day and night, and understand the significance of buoys of the IALA system

2. Knows sources of information on: Local regulations, port entry and departure signals, VTS and Port Operations Radio

3. Can plan a harbour entry/departure, taking account of possible presence of large vessels and avoiding navigational hazards

These aspects are discussed in section C of the book.

PRACTICAL ELEMENTS (ALL CANDIDATES)

1. Start
- Give safety briefing including use of safety equipment
- Has listened to weather forecasts
- Pre-start engine checks
- Use kill cord (if fitted)
- Start engine
- Check cooling
- Knows fuel range.

2. Depart from Pontoon
- Understands use of springs to depart from leeward wall/pontoon
- Communicate with crew
- Position fenders correctly

3. 360-degree turn in Confined Space

4. Securing to Buoy
- Communicate effectively with the crew
- Prepare warp
- Choose correct angle of approach
- Control speed of approach
- Secure boat effectively
- Depart from the mooring safely

5. Man Overboard
- Observe the MOB or instruct crew to do so
- Demonstrate correct direction and speed of approach
- Make suitable contact with MOB

6a. Planing-speed Manoeuvres (if appropriate)
- Choose suitable area

- Show awareness of other water users
- Warn crew before each manoeuvre
- Look around before S and U turns
- Control speed on U turns

6b. Handling under Sail (if appropriate)
- Sail triangular course with one leg to windward.
- Choose suitable area for hoisting/ lowering sails
- Use sails suitable for prevailing conditions
- Show awareness of wind direction
- Trim sails correctly on each point of sailing
- Warn crew before manoeuvres
- Look round before tacking or gybing
- Control sails when tacking and gybing

7. Coming alongside Windward Pontoon
- Communicate effectively with crew
- Show awareness of other water users
- Prepare warps and fenders
- Choose correct angle of approach
- Control speed of approach
- Stop boat in place required and secure to pontoon
- Stop engine

This part of the syllabus is discussed in section 4 of the book.

■ APPLYING FOR YOUR FIRST ICC

To obtain an ICC, you must complete an ICC Application Form in full and sign the declaration.

This should be sent to the RYA Certification Department, together with:

■ a passport sized photograph (with your name on the reverse)

■ proof that your nationality or your country of residence make you eligible to be issued with a UK ICC issued by the RYA

■ evidence of your competence (relevant sections of the application form have been signed to say you have passed the ICC assessment or the ICC CEVNI Test or photocopies of any certificates you are presenting as evidence are enclosed

■ payment (including the fast track fee if required) – the ICC is issued to RYA Members free of charge

■ RENEWING AN ICC

The ICC is valid for 5 years. Unless you wish to have additional categories added to your ICC, the renewal process is simply a paper exercise.

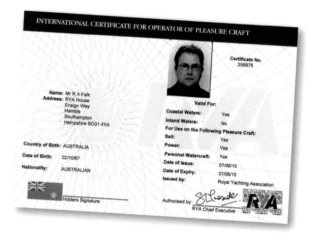

The remainder of this book is split into four parts. Parts A, B and C are the oral or written tests, and the fourth part is a practical boat handling test.

Part A is relevant to all ICC assessment candidates and covers some essential regulations plus safety.

Part B is relevant to the CEVNI test and is for Inland candidates only. The test comprises a written, multiple choice answer paper on CEVNI.

Part C is relevant to the ICC assessment and covers more regulations, pilotage and navigation for coastal candidates. Parts A and C may be written papers or oral questioning by the assessor throughout the progress of the test.

Part 4 is the practical boat handling test for all ICC assessment candidates.

PART A: ALL CANDIDATES – REGULATIONS

1. Knows responsibility for keeping a proper lookout.
2. Can determine a 'safe speed'.
3. Can recognise a potential collision situation.
4. Can identify 'give way' vessel in a collision situation.
5. Knows what action to take as 'give way' and 'stand on' vessel.
6. Knows responsibilities of small boat in a narrow channel.
7. Can recognise manoeuvring signals (1,2,3 & 5 short blasts)
8. Can make and recognise visual distress signals.

The International Regulations for the Prevention of Collision at Sea (IRPCS)
With the exception of inshore waters where local bylaws apply, there are no rigid restrictions laying down where you can and cannot go and how you get there. There are however, a series of rules governing the operation of boats and how you must act when in proximity with other vessels and where the risk of collision exists. These are the IRPCS (Col Regs) and they are mandatory for all. You are breaking the law if you fail to comply.

The full IRPCS is a fairly meaty document, but the basic rules are quite simple. For instance, the regulations say that:

1. YOU MUST MAINTAIN A PROPER LOOKOUT AT ALL TIMES BY ALL AVAILABLE MEANS

Available means are sight, sound, and radar/AIS if you have it. This is a sensible rule. On sailboats you may have to move around a little to keep watch on blind spots behind sails and rigging. All boaters should be in the habit of looking all around (not just forward) especially before manoeuvring.

2. YOU MUST ALWAYS NAVIGATE AT A SAFE SPEED

You should proceed at a speed that allows you time to think and take proper avoiding action. In open waters you can go as fast as you like but in confined harbours, heavy traffic, poor visibility or shallow water you must slow down. You should take care that your wash or wake is not likely to cause difficulty to any other water users.

3. IT IS EVERYONE'S RESPONSIBILITY TO AVOID COLLISION

Most situations involve 'stand on' and 'give way' vessels where the latter has the major responsibility to take action. However that doesn't mean the stand on vessel can plough on regardless. There may come a time when the stand on vessel must act to avoid hitting another vessel – as required in the IRPCS. When it comes to collisions no one is entirely blameless.

To avoid collisions you first have to recognise that a risk exists. Sometimes it's obvious – head to head for example. Often it's not. A good check is to take a compass bearing of the other vessel. If it remains constant over a short period of time, you are either on parallel courses or if the distance between you is reducing you are converging towards a point where you will collide. Several methods can be used to establish the bearing: a hand bearing compass, sighting in relation to part of your boat's structure, or periodically checking the other vessel's range and bearing on radar.

4. AVOIDING ACTION SHALL BE TIMELY AND OBVIOUS

The earlier the better is the rule for taking avoiding action, but don't just turn a couple of degrees. This may solve the problem as far as you are concerned, but the move may not be obvious to the other vessel. Always make bold gestures so that the other party can see the steps you have taken. At night that gesture will have to be bold enough to change the light aspect that you are showing the other vessel. A sound signal may also be useful. (see page 15)

5. PASSING RULES

MOTOR VESSELS HEAD TO HEAD ▶

This is the only situation that requires action from both vessels. Each must alter their course to starboard so that the other passes down their port side.

▼ MOTOR VESSELS ON CONVERGING COURSES

The give way vessel is the one that has the other on its starboard side. Either slow down and let the stand on vessel pass ahead or alter course to starboard and drop around her stern.

However, if you are the stand on vessel and avoiding action has been left too late, turn to starboard. **Never turn to port in an attempt to go around the other vessels stern**. The give way vessel might belatedly turn to starboard and a head on collision could occur. By turning away, the impact will be delayed and its force reduced.

Give way vessel

5. PASSING RULES (continued)

SAILING VESSELS OPPOSITE TACKS ▶

The sailboat with wind on its port side should give way. If sails are set on both sides then it's the mainsail that determines which tack it is on.

◀ SAILING VESSELS SAME TACK

When two converging yachts are on the same tack, the vessel to windward should give way.

OVERTAKING ▶

You are considered to be 'overtaking' if you approach another vessel within the sector of its stern light, and you remain 'the overtaking vessel' until you are clear ahead. This applies if you are in a sailboat overtaking a power vessel, if you are fast enough to overtake it's up to you to take the avoiding action.

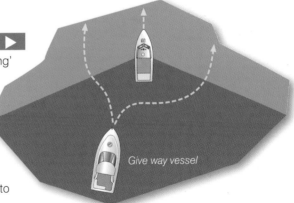

POWER GIVES WAY TO SAIL – BUT NOT ALWAYS

As long as a power driven vessel is under command, not being overtaken, constrained by its draught or otherwise restricted in its ability to manoeuvre – such as fishing, trawling, towing etc – it shall give way to sailing vessels. It's worth mentioning that the IRPCS only recognises power driven vessels or sailing vessels. There's no category for motor-sailers. If a sailboat has her engine running and in gear, for the purposes of the regulations she is a power driven vessel, even if she has sails hoisted.

6. NARROW CHANNELS

Rule 9 governs conduct in narrow channels and is widely misunderstood and abused. Skippers of small boats need to bear the following three parts of the rule in mind:

1. Vessels should navigate as close as is safely possible to the edge of the channel on their starboard side. That makes good sense and makes it easier for vessels to pass 'port to port.'

2. Vessels less than 20m. long and sailing vessels shall not impede the progress of vessels that can only navigate safely along the channel. There are often areas outside main channels where we small boat skippers can navigate well away from the larger ships. Make use of those areas and use the 'small boat channels' if they are available.

3. A vessel shall not cross a channel if such crossing impedes the progress of a vessel who can only navigate within the channel. Those vessels 'constrained by their draught' might well include deep draught sailing yachts and motor cruisers so be careful whenever you want to cross a channel.

7. MANOEUVRING SIGNALS

Sound signals used to alert others to your intended manoeuvres.

● ONE SHORT BLAST: "I intend to turn to starboard"

● ● TWO SHORT BLASTS: "I intend to turn to port"

● ● ● THREE SHORT BLASTS: "I am engaging stern propulsion" (meaning an intention to go astern though this may not be apparent at the time.)

They can also be used as a warning.

● ● ● ● ● FIVE OR MORE SHORT BLASTS: "I do not understand your intentions" or "you may not have taken sufficient avoiding action"

▬▬ ONE LONG BLAST: Sounded by a vessel nearing a bend to warn others who may be obscured behind it

8. VISUAL DISTRESS SIGNALS

Skippers should know and recognise visual distress signals so that they can take the appropriate action, or indeed use one themselves. Internationally recognised signals are:

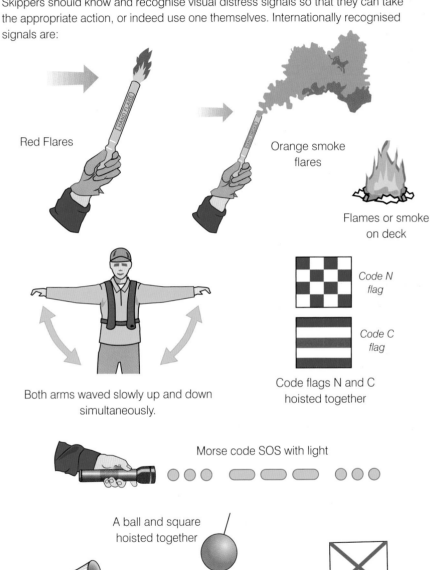

Red Flares

Orange smoke flares

Flames or smoke on deck

Code N flag

Code C flag

Code flags N and C hoisted together

Both arms waved slowly up and down simultaneously.

Morse code SOS with light

A ball and square hoisted together

Morse code SOS with sound or loud continuous urgent noise

Code flag V isn't a distress signal but means 'I require assistance'.

PART A: ALL CANDIDATES – SAFETY

1. Is able to use and instruct crew in the use of:
   - Lifejackets
   - Distress flares
   - Fire extinguishers
   - Kill cord (if fitted)

2. Can prepare a boat for use and take sensible precautions before setting out including:
   - Engine checks
   - Check fuel for range/duration of trip
   - Avoid overloading boat
   - Obtain weather forecast

■ LIFEJACKETS AND HARNESSES

Modern lifejackets are compact and comfortable and more and more sailors are sensibly taking the decision to wear one at all times. When buying one for yourself or wearing one belonging to the boat, check it is self-inflating or manual. Also, check that it has the correct buoyancy rating for your body weight.

Deflated   *Inflated*

Most lifejackets are now combined with harnesses. Sailboat crew should tether themselves to the boat in rough weather, fog or at night. The tether should be long enough to reach from your harness to your feet plus a few centimetres, so that you can walk comfortably along the side deck with the tether sliding on a jack stay. But not so long that you could be dragged underwater if you go overboard. It's a good idea to secure the tether onto the high side of a heeled sailboat so that a fall will leave you on deck rather than over the leeward rail. Clips on tethers should be of an approved type, or they can be prone to accidentally 'tripping' open when used on metal 'D' rings.

Some countries insist on the use of lifejackets at all times for certain classes of vessel, so check local regulations when sailing abroad.

Approved type safety hook

LIFEJACKETS OR BUOYANCY AIDS SHOULD BE WORN:

1. If you are a non-swimmer and there is any possibility of entering the water
2. When the skipper deems it necessary
3. When abandoning ship
4. When you feel you want to wear one or if you are not totally sure that you do not need to wear one

■ DISTRESS FLARES

Always read the manufacturer's instructions and store in a waterproof container.

There are several different types of flare for marine use.

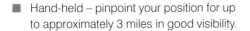

- ■ Hand-held – pinpoint your position for up to approximately 3 miles in good visibility.

- ■ Rocket or Parachute – can be seen for up to fifteen miles in good visibility. Not good in low cloud when they should be fired at 45° to the horizon.

- ■ Smoke

Fire all flares downwind, from the leeward side of the boat

They come in three colours:

- ■ Red – for signalling distress.
  Difficult to see in bright sunshine when orange should be used.

- ■ White – to attract attention and avoid collision

- ■ Orange – for signalling in distress in bright sunshine.

When firing a flare

1. Never fire a rocket or parachute flare near to a helicopter.

2. Wear gloves when firing and do not look directly into the flare.

3. Fire downwind from the leeward side which will take smoke and sparks away from the boat and crew.

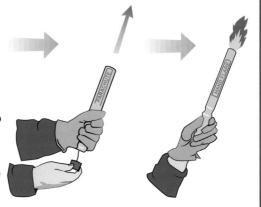

4. Fire a series of flares at short intervals because the first may not have been seen.

5. All flares have a "use by date" so check flare dates regularly.

■ FIRE EXTINGUISHERS

- ■ Dry Powder – most common type found on small craft. Suitable for most fires including engine fires. Never to be used on burning liquid.
- ■ Fire Blanket or Foam – for burning liquid.
- ■ Automatic Inert Gas – Best for fires in the engine space. Another idea is to have a small keyhole opening which will allow the use of a hand-held extinguisher without the need to open up the engine space.

Engine fires can be extinguished through small access ports

In general, place extinguishers near potential hazard areas and where the crew can get to them. For instance place a fire blanket near to the galley but not over the stove which could be ablaze.

Where possible, direct the extinguishant at the base of a fire and keep firing until you are sure that the fire is out. You may not get a second squeeze out of an extinguisher. Some discharge till empty once triggered.

And remember: all extinguishers must be serviced regularly, otherwise they may not work when you need them.

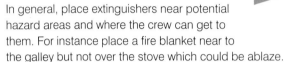

	paper	chemical	electrical
WATER	✓	✗	✗
FOAM	✓	✓	✗
DRY POWDER ABC type	✓	✓	✓
BC type	✗	✓	✓
CO$_2$	✗	✓	✓

NOTE: Halon extinguishers have been banned for environmental reasons but substitutes are available. Contact the manufacturers.

■ KILL CORDS

Kill cords must be worn by helms of small power craft, RIBs, etc. Boats, running amok, out of control, have caused damage, serious injury and sometimes death. The kill cord is what it says, a light line providing a fixed link between the driver and the engine.

If the driver moves too far away from the engine controls, a key will be pulled, the ignition switched off, thereby killing the engine. It is recommended that the kill cord be attached around the leg or a strong point on the helmsman's personal buoyancy.

■ ENGINE CHECKS

Good skippers will be in the habit of making some basic engine checks every time before they go to sea. Checks only take a minute or two but could save you from embarrassment, inconvenience, or worse.

They should include:

BEFORE STARTING

1. Make a visual inspection around engine and bilge for oil, water or fuel leaks.
2. Make sure that oil and cooling water levels are at the correct levels.
3. Examine drive belts for wear and tension.

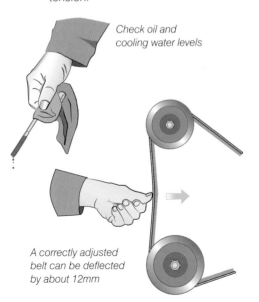

Check oil and cooling water levels

A correctly adjusted belt can be deflected by about 12mm

AFTER STARTING

1. Check the exhaust for flow of raw cooling water.
2. Monitor gauges and panel lights to make sure that batteries are charging and engine temperature stays within the correct range.
3. On outboard engines look for the tell tale cooling jet.

■ RANGE AND SPARE FUEL

All skippers going to sea – not just power boaters – should check the amount of fuel they are carrying and relate that to their potential range under power. Carrying spare fuel in a separate tank is a good idea in case of contamination of the main supply or blockages in the main tank supply hoses. Planing boat owners should consider their range when heavy seas force them into displacement mode. In such conditions speeds will drop considerably while the fuel consumptions may well rise. The fuel consumption of your engine at various engine speeds should be shown in your engine manual. Learn how your fuel consumption varies in practice, taking account of loaded weight and weather conditions.

■ OVERLOADING

Overloading boats with movable weights – such as people! – is dangerous, since to do so can have seriously detrimental effects on stability. Most at risk are flat bottomed, planing, motorboats. Without the benefit of a deep ballast keel, they can easily be tipped over by their occupants rushing from side to side. Boats built since the introduction of the European Recreational Craft Directive (RCD) in 1998 will be badged with a recommended maximum crew and baggage allowance.

The most obvious abuses of loading limits are witnessed in harbours, when large crews crowd ashore in small tenders.

The lessons are:
1. Never overload any craft.
2. Ensure all occupants are wearing lifejackets.
3. If returning after dark carry a light to identify yourself to other vessels.

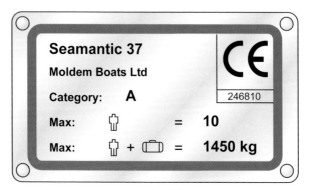

The Builder's Plate should tell you how many people and baggage a boat can safely carry.

■ WEATHER FORECASTS

Weather forecasts are easy to obtain, and usually very accurate when it comes to predicting wind strength and direction, temperature etc.

There are many sources, including:

- ■ The internet gives access to many sites including the Met Office.
- ■ Local Radio Stations usually broadcast hourly.
- ■ SMS messages can be directed to our mobile phones.
- ■ Recorded telephone services are available.
- ■ Forecast displayed in the harbour office window.

There really is no excuse for going to sea without a forecast and once at sea the Coastguard makes regular broadcasts of weather information on VHF radio.

Good they might be but we should appreciate their shortcomings, particularly with regard to the sea state. Look at the problem the meteorologist faces when forecasting wave sizes. He starts with a perfectly sound scientific appraisal of what the wind is doing but is then asked to come up with a one-word description of the sea state for a long stretch of coast and up to 12 miles offshore. That sea area will include sheltered bays, exposed headlands with shallow ledges and – worse still – tidal streams of variable velocity that will change direction through 180° within the forecast period. He can't possibly describe the conditions in every location so takes a general view of the sea state in open water created by the wind alone.

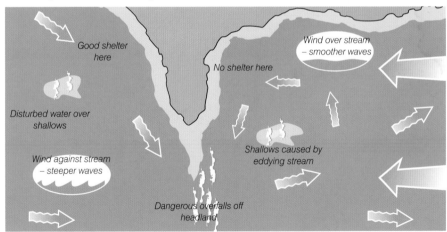

No forecast can predict what the conditions might be like from place to place

Let's say that the forecaster gives us a Force 5 wind and a moderate sea state. We must look at that prediction of wave height objectively and realise that, while we might find calmer conditions in the lee of the land, we might encounter dangerously rough seas in the overfalls off a headland, when the stream runs against the wind. It's up to each skipper to make seamanlike judgements and then plan his passage to suit his own prediction of the sea conditions and his boat's and crew's ability to handle them.

■ Understands CEVNI (European Inland Waterways Regulations)

The Code Européen des Voies de Navigation Intérieure (CEVNI) is a resolution of the United Nations Economic Commission for Europe Inland Transport Committee that provides harmonised rules and signs designed to ensure safety on the interconnected European inland waterways. The resolution is under constant review by the Working Party on Inland Water Transport. The fifth revision of CEVNI was published in the summer of 2015. In order to bring them into force, the rules are adopted by national governments and the four River Commissions into the regulations that apply for their area of authority.

The main European international rivers are managed by specially established inter-Governmental River Commissions entrusted with setting technical and legal standards for their respective river networks. In each country, as in the UK, there may be one or more navigation authorities responsible for implementing their rules within their jurisdiction.

It takes time for the changes to be made to the national, local, and River Commission regulations which bring CEVNI into force. While this book is based on the fifth revision of CEVNI, the rules in force may be based on a previous version. However, the rules in force may not exactly match the relevant revision of CEVNI, as some elements of CEVNI may not be appropriate for the local conditions and there is scope for the implementing navigation authority to alter the rules to suit.

It is the rules in force which will indicate the area in which the rules apply, and which, if you are coming from the sea, will indicate where you change over from adhering to the COLREGs. However, if you are seeing CEVNI signage it will be a good indicator that you are on an inland waterway.

The rules in force may include a requirement to carry a copy of those rules on board. In most cases the rules are not published in English, but that neither negates the requirement to carry them nor provides an excuse for not being aware of your obligations. There may also be inland waters where the local rules are not based on the CEVNI resolution and a completely different set of rules may be in force.

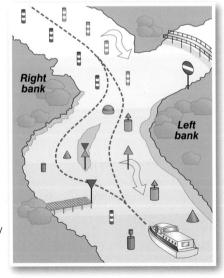

If you are familiar with the COLREGs you will find that many of the regulations are the same as at sea: the passing rules for motor and sailing vessels of a similar size, for instance, and the buoyage system is basically the same. You may even find cardinal marks on wider waterways and lakes.

Banks of the waterways are named 'right' and 'left' from the standpoint of facing downstream, regardless of whichever way you are proceeding. The right bank generally has red buoys and the left bank green buoys. This marking is very familiar to tidewater sailors entering inland waterways – when going upstream, you will find red buoys on your port side (against the right bank) and green to starboard (against the left bank).

Pleasure vessels under 20 metres LOA are designated as 'Small Craft'. Other vessels, mainly commercial craft, are 'Normal Vessels'. In general, on lakes, the offshore IRPCS apply, but on rivers and canals Small Craft must keep clear of Normal Vessels. In order to keep clear effectively you must understand the actions of the Normal Vessels and also the rules and the meaning of the signs, etc.

Here are a few pointers:

■ On rivers and canals, boats heading upstream give way to vessels heading downstream, and the convention is that they will pass 'port to port'. If, however, the upstream boat wants the downstream vessel to pass on starboard then she will place a scintillating white light or a blue board on her starboard side.

■ Deep water channels in rivers are not always in the middle of the waterway and you will find deep draught vessels crossing over from one bank towards the other as they seek the deep water. The crossovers are marked by various signs (see below). Keep a look out for them so that you can both avoid running aground and anticipate the actions of other vessels.

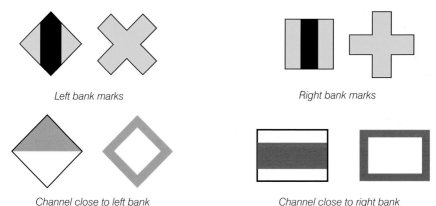

Left bank marks

Right bank marks

Channel close to left bank

Channel close to right bank

■ Restricted zones, for bathing or water skiing for instance, will be marked by lines of yellow buoys. As far as possible the nature of the restriction will be indicated by signs on the bank. Zones where navigation is prohibited will be marked by yellow buoys with red pennants on top.

It's really the signs, both on the banks and on moving vessels that are the biggest unknown for newcomers to the waterways.

The signs fall into seven categories:

1. PROHIBITIONS

Red or Red and White signs, often red borders with a red diagonal stripe. These are actions that you must not take. In many cases the subject of the prohibition is obvious from the sign.

No entry

No entry except for non-motorised craft

No overtaking

No passing or overtaking (effectively one-way traffic)

No berthing within the breadth indicated in metres (measured from the sign)

No anchoring or trailing of anchors, cables or chains

No mooring

No turning

Do not create wash

No sport or pleasure craft

No water skiing

No windsurfing

Motorised craft prohibited

No sailing vessels

No manually propelled craft

No personal watercraft

No speeding sportsboats

No launching or beaching

2. OTHER TRAFFIC LIGHTS

Lights are used both to provide information and to control the movement of traffic.

   or   Isophase (equal on and off)

- A pair of flashing yellow lights (sometimes only one in France) warn that a vessel is coming out of a port or sidearm. Traffic on the main waterway must alter course or speed accordingly.
- A single flashing yellow means entry into that port is forbidden.
- Two means you can enter but with great caution.

It is recommended that you steer from the fixed white light towards the isophase flashing one

  or

Stop as required by the regulations

  or

You may proceed

  or   plus   or  or

Passage through movable bridges is controlled by red and green lights. If yellow lights are shown at the same time as one or two reds, passage is permitted for vessels of reduced height. One yellow light signifies two-way traffic. Two yellows signify one-way traffic.

3. MANDATORY

These red bordered signs give instructions that must be followed.

Go in direction of arrow

Move to the side of the channel on your port side

Keep to the side of the channel on your port side

Cross channel to port (a similar, reversed sign would indicate it crossing to starboard)

Stop as necessary

Do not exceed speed indicated

Give a sound signal

Do not enter or cross the main waterway unless certain this will not oblige vessels proceeding on it to change their course or speed

Keep listening watch on VHF channel indicated

4. RESTRICTIONS

Other red bordered signs provide important information of physical limitations ahead.

Depth of water limited

Width of passage or channel limited

Headroom limited

The channel lies at a distance from the right/left bank: the figure indicates the distance in metres from the sign vessels should keep

5. RECOMMENDATIONS

These signal the best way to proceed. Other options are at your own risk.

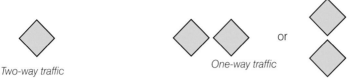

Two-way traffic

One-way traffic

or

Recommended spans through a fixed bridge may be marked with yellow diamonds (occasionally yellow lights). Craft using unmarked spans do so at their own risk. If you see two yellows, it means one-way in your favour. There will be a 'no entry' sign on the other side.

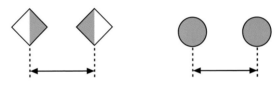

It is recommended you keep within the space indicated

It is recommended that you
follow the arrow

6. AUTHORISATIONS

Green signs, flags or lights indicate an authorisation to pass.

7. INDICATIONS

Blue and white signs can both provide information and indicate that certain activities are permitted.

Overhead cable

Weir

Ferry not operating independently

Self propelled ferry

Berthing permitted

Berthing permitted within lateral distance indicated

Berthing permitted within a lateral distance out from the sign

Maximum number of craft permitted to berth abreast

Anchoring permitted

Sports or pleasure boats permitted

Sailing vessels permitted

Water skiing permitted

This waterway is considered to be a tributary of the waterway you are approaching

The waterway being approached is considered a tributary to this waterway

Turning permitted

Mooring permitted

You will find certain daymarks and lights on vessels that you will not find at sea.
Here's a selection that you should be able to recognise:

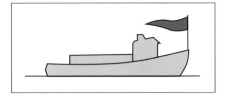

Vessel with priority.

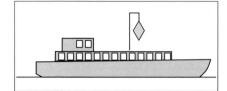

Passenger vessel up to 20m.

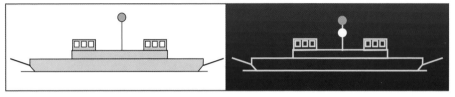

Ferries not independent.

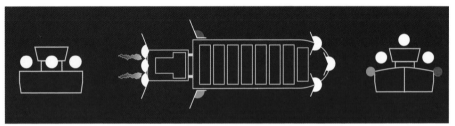

Pushed convoy.

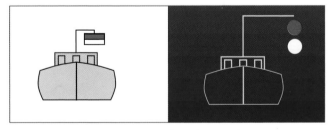

Vessels protected against wash.

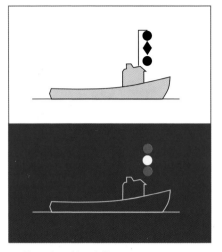

Restricted in ability to manoeuvre.

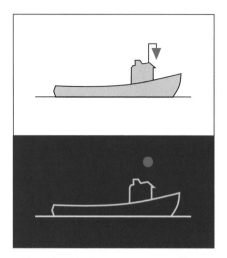

Vessels with dangerous cargo. There can be up to three blue lights or shapes depending upon the nature of the danger.

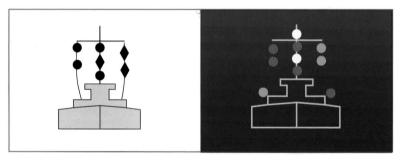

Vessel restricted in its ability to manoeuvre. Pass to port.

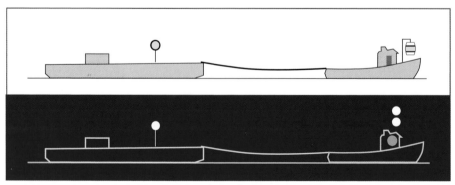

Tug leading towed convoy.

- Knows the rules relating to traffic separation schemes.
- Knows requirements for navigation lights and shapes to be displayed by own vessel.
- Can recognise the following from the lights: power driven, sailing vessel, vessel at anchor, tug and tow, fishing vessel, dredger.
- Knows sound signals to be made in reduced visibility by vessels in question 3.

■ TRAFFIC SEPARATION SCHEMES

In heavy traffic areas and around major headlands there's a very serious risk of collision between large commercial vessels. To separate and regulate the flows of traffic, authorities have introduced Traffic Separation Schemes (TSS). These are effectively 'corridors' through which large ships moving in one direction must pass. One corridor is reserved for ships moving in one direction, with another adjacent corridor for those moving in the opposite direction. The two corridors are separated by a 'no go' zone, coloured in magenta on the chart. Vessels, including sailing yachts, crossing a 'TSS' must give way to ships moving through it. Operations such as dredging, fishing, anchoring etc. are not allowed in a TSS. Small vessels should avoid TSS when ever possible, but if they have to cross, they must do so at a sensible speed, and with their 'heading' at 90° to the flow of traffic so that they quit the TSS as rapidly as possible.

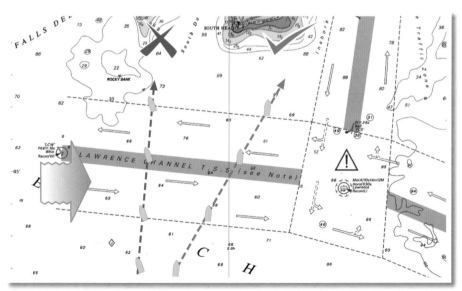

Crossing a TSS

■ NAVIGATION LIGHTS AND SHAPES

All vessels underway must show running lights during the hours of darkness. Running lights comprise three lights of different colours showing in three sectors as shown right. In addition, when a vessel is power driven it must show a white 'steaming light' over the red and green running light sectors.

Small boats under 7m. long and not capable of exceeding 7 knots need only show a single all round white light. Small boats without any power need only show a white light in the direction of oncoming boats.

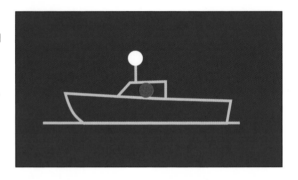

all-round 360°
masthead light 225°
starboard 112.5°
port 112.5°
stern light 135°
towing light 135°

In addition to port and starboard lights, power vessels less than 50m. must show a white masthead light and stern light. Vessels of less than 12m. can combine these two in a single all-round white as shown here.

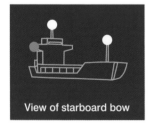

View of starboard bow

View of port bow

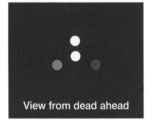

View from dead ahead

Motor vessels over 50m. LOA must show a second white steaming light above and behind the first.

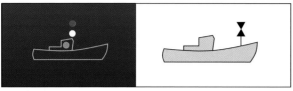

A vessel engaged in fishing displays an additional all-round red light above its white light. Two cones apex together by day.

Sailboats under sail and under 20m. LOA may put all three running lights in one unit at the masthead. (Tricolour light).

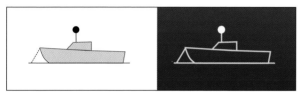

Vessel at anchor.

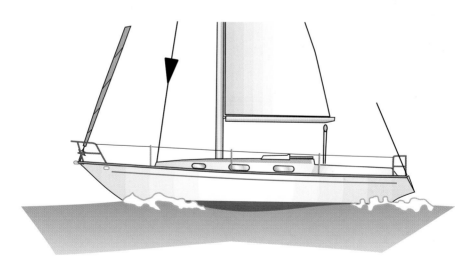

Sailing boats motoring with sails hoisted must show an inverted cone over their foredeck, to show other water users that they are a 'motor driven vessel'.

■ SPECIAL LIGHTS, DAY SHAPES AND SOUND SIGNALS

When vessels are compromised in their ability to take proper avoiding action, they must make a declaration to that effect using: shapes in daylight, additional lights at night and sound signals in reduced visibility. If they do, then we must all give way to them, whether we are under sail or motor.

Here are some common ones you should learn to recognise:

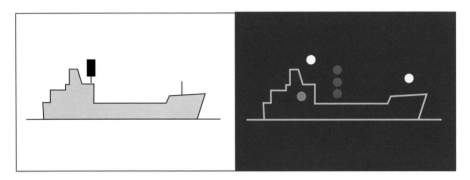

If constrained by draught, three all-round red lights in a vertical line are displayed, as well as the usual lights if under way. The day shape is a black cylinder.

Fog: ▬▬ ● ● every two minutes.

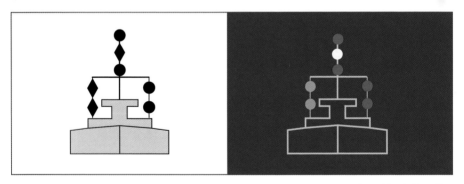

Dredgers show the same vertical red, white, red lights as vessels restricted in their ability to manoeuvre, plus two vertical reds and two vertical greens at either side. The green lights indicate which side is safe to pass. Day shapes are, again, the same as RAM, plus two balls and two diamonds indicating the safe side at either side.

Fog: ▬▬ ● ● every two minutes.

Towing less than 200m: Along with the usual power vessel lights, the tug carries a second white masthead light and a yellow towing light above the sternlight and displaying over the same arc. The tow shows sidelights and sternlight.

Towing over 200m: As above but with a third masthead light.
Fog: ▬ ● ● every two minutes.

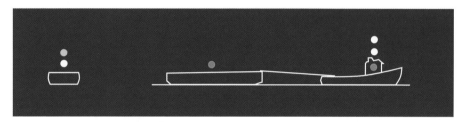

Towing less than 200m

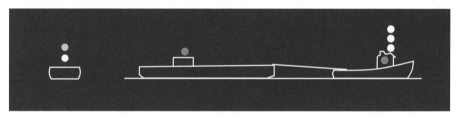

Towing over 200m

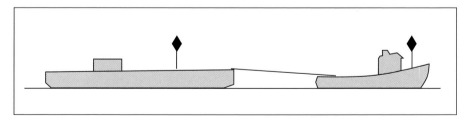

By day tug and tow each show a black diamond shape.

- Can recognise by day and night, and understand the significance of buoys of the IALA system.
- Knows sources of information on: Local regulations, port entry and departure signals, VTS and Port Operations Radio.

- Can plan a harbour entry/ departure, taking account of possible presence of large vessels and avoiding navigational hazards.

■ NAVIGATION MARKS AND BUOYS

In the mid 1970s the International Association of Lighthouse Authorities (IALA) established the first unified system of buoyage. There are two IALA regions, 'B', comprises North America, parts of South America and the Caribbean, plus one or two other countries that follow the American tradition, while 'A' is the rest of the world. For the purposes of the ICC we are only interested in European waters and so will concentrate on IALA region A.

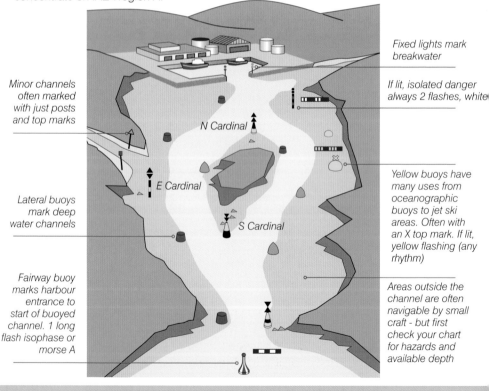

Fixed lights mark breakwater

Minor channels often marked with just posts and top marks

If lit, isolated danger always 2 flashes, white

N Cardinal

E Cardinal

Lateral buoys mark deep water channels

S Cardinal

Yellow buoys have many uses from oceanographic buoys to jet ski areas. Often with an X top mark. If lit, yellow flashing (any rhythm)

Fairway buoy marks harbour entrance to start of buoyed channel. 1 long flash isophase or morse A

Areas outside the channel are often navigable by small craft - but first check your chart for hazards and available depth

LATERAL MARKS

Lateral marks define channels, the basic two marks are the Port Hand and Starboard Hand. They can be buoys or beacons (posts) but will define the appropriate channel edge when you are facing in the 'Direction of Buoyage'.

The direction of buoyage can be defined as the direction of the flood tide, but where that situation is confused or where there is any doubt, look at your chart. You should find this symbol (left) to show the proper direction.

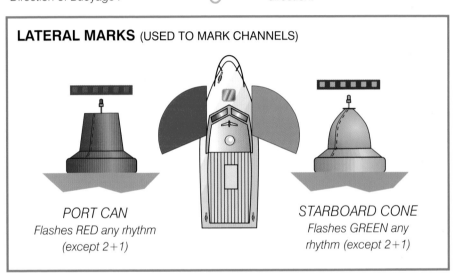

LATERAL MARKS (USED TO MARK CHANNELS)

PORT CAN
Flashes RED any rhythm
(except 2+1)

STARBOARD CONE
Flashes GREEN any
rhythm (except 2+1)

There are three more common lateral marks that you should know:

1. THE 'SPECIAL' MARK

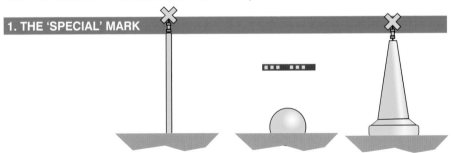

These marks have no navigational significance. They are used as race buoys, to define swimming or water-skiing zones, firing ranges.

They can be all sorts of shapes, but they are always yellow and often have a St. Andrew's Cross as a top mark. If lit, it will be with a yellow light.

2. THE ISOLATED DANGER MARK

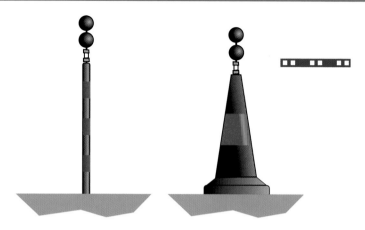

These marks are used to mark a relatively small hazard in the middle of an area of open water and can be passed on either side, but not too close as the mark is set on the hazard. They can be buoys, beacons, or even concrete pillars but they are always painted with red and black hoops with two black balls on top. If they are lit it will be with a white light flashing in groups of two.

3. SAFE WATER MARK

Sometimes called a 'Fairway Buoy' or 'Sea Buoy' they are striped vertically red and white, have a single ball on top and will flash a single long white flash every ten seconds. These buoys are usually set in safe, deep water at the seaward end of fairways, or harbour approach channels. Traditionally they are the 'point of departure' and then the waypoints to aim for, and mark the transition from open water navigation to pilotage.

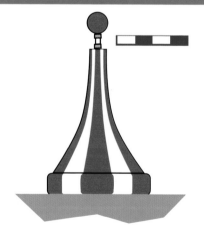

CARDINAL BUOYS

Cardinal buoys and beacons mark hazards. There are four types and though their construction may vary their colours, top marks and lights follow a consistent pattern.

Cardinal marks are used in isolation or in groups to mark off lying hazards. They can also be combined with lateral marks to provide a comprehensive marking system in harbours as shown on page 38. To stay in safe water go:

- North of a North Cardinal.
- East of an East Cardinal.
- West of a West Cardinal.
- South of a South Cardinal.

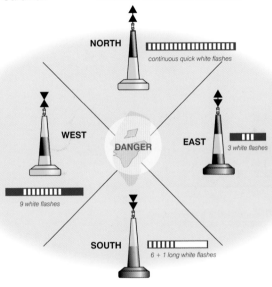

■ SOURCES OF INFORMATION

Along with detailed charts, almanacs and pilot books provide a wealth of useful information when entering and leaving port, or making coastal passages.

Pilot books give very detailed descriptions of harbours etc. and suggested pilot plans for entry. Some have photographs, which can make recognition of landmarks much easier. It should be noted, however, that some information in pilot books may often be out of date even before they complete the publishing process. So be wary.

Almanacs are published annually and although the information they contain is abbreviated, it will be current. They contain lots more than just pilotage notes. For example, they publish the 'Port Operations' or 'VTS' VHF channels. It's worth monitoring these radio channels to be aware of large commercial ship movements.

Shop online at
www.rya.org.uk/shop

- Secure online ordering
- 15% discount for RYA members
- Books, DVDs, navigation aids and lots more
- Free delivery to a UK address for RYA members on orders over £25
- Free delivery to an overseas address for RYA members on orders over £50
- Buying online from the RYA shop enables the RYA in its work on behalf of its members

■ HARBOUR ENTRY/EXIT PLANS

Before approaching a new harbour prepare a plan for the entry. If the system of buoys is comprehensive, the plan may well be a simple list of the marks that you need to pass, but you should note down the 'headings' you expect to take between marks to ensure that you have identified them correctly.

Sectored lights may occur in sequence to lead you safely in

If there are cross tides – often the case – or at night when navigation mark lights may be lost against background shore lights, your plans should be more sophisticated and include all of the aids that the harbour authority has provided.

Those aids may include:

Transits – two objects (lights) placed on an extension of the ideal approach heading which, when brought into line one behind the other, indicate the safe route in.

Directional lights – these lights are screened so that they only show over a limited arc. They are often sectored so that they will appear: white when on line, red if you've strayed to the left and green if you go too far right.

You can also set up our own guidance systems:

LEADING BEARINGS

When making a straight line approach towards an identifiable object, use your hand bearing compass. Check that you're on the safe approach line, and then drive down it, steering to keep the bearing constant.

CLEARING BEARINGS

If you have to tack towards an object you can run 'clearing bearings' back from the objects on the limits of the safe approach. Stay between the clearing bearings and you will be in safe water.

EXAMPLE 1

It's night. There's a westerly wind. The chart below shows a pilot plan for entry to Blackmill Marina, coming in from the east around Iguana Point.

We've already checked that our mast, height 12 metres, will pass under the road bridge and overhead cables.

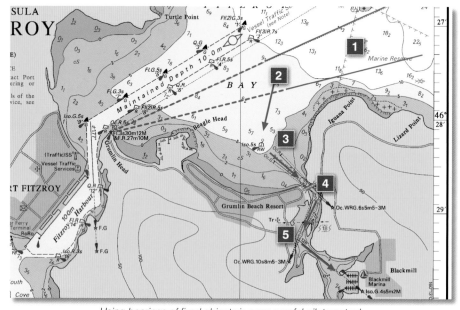

Using bearings of fixed objects is a very useful pilotage tool

1. Having identified the lighthouse on Grumlin Head, our skipper tacks towards it keeping the bearing less than 264° but more the 253° magnetic.

2. When the 'safe water' buoy off Grumlin Beach bears 200° magnetic, he steers directly towards it.

3. At the buoy he turns the boat onto a heading of 136° magnetic, identifies the Occulting 6 sec. light ahead and steers to stay in the white sector.

4. Passing under the road bridge, he looks to his right to identify the Occulting 10 sec. light, passes through the green sector and turns towards it as it changes to white. He then checks that his heading is roughly 211° magnetic.

5. After a mile, he looks to his left to identify the Isophase 4 sec. transit lights, and when the white appears directly over the green, he turns onto 135° keeping the two lights in line to the marina.

EXAMPLE 2

The chart below shows a pilot plan for Hamilton Marina. Our skipper has noted the transits set up on the first two legs but is not confident of either his ability to identify them in daylight or the quality of visibility when he arrives. So he takes a few minutes to put the positions of the major turns into his GPS as waypoints W1 – W4.

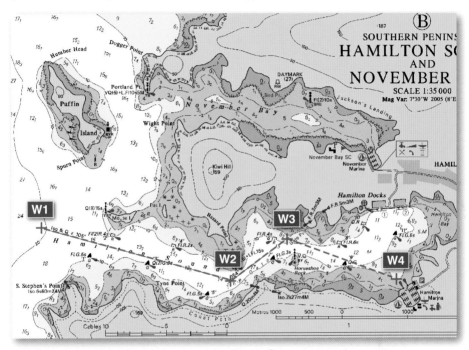

For tricky pilotage use waypoints with care. Some charts are inaccurate.

On arrival at Waypoint 1 he can now ask his GPS for the bearing and distance to Waypoint 2.

Checking that the bearing is the 105° that the chart shows he can now proceed confidently to Waypoint 2 steering to keep the bearing a constant 105°.

Repeating the process at the next two turns he will arrive safely at the marina even in poor visibility.

PART C: ADDITIONALLY FOR CANDIDATES FOR COASTAL WATERS – NAVIGATION

- Interpret a navigational chart, understand the significance of charted depths and drying heights and can identify charted hazards.
- Plot position by cross bearings and by Lat/Long.
- Determine a magnetic course to steer, making allowances for leeway and tidal stream.

- Can use a tide table to find the times and heights of high and low water at a standard port.
- Determine the direction and rate of a tidal stream from a tidal stream atlas or tidal diamonds on a chart.
- Understands the basic use of a GPS/Chart Plotter.

The correct interpretation of navigational charts is vital. Charts are covered in symbols some of which are quite obscure. The Key to chart symbols is an Admiralty publication called 'Chart 5011'.

Here are some important symbols that you should know.

Dangerous underwater rock

Rock which covers and uncovers

Rock awash at the level of chart datum

Wreck showing above chart datum

Dangerous wreck

Wreck swept to depth shown

Underwater cables

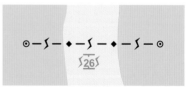

Power transmission line, showing safe clearance

Visitors moorings

◼ CHARTED DEPTHS AND DRYING HEIGHTS

Colour schemes of charts vary depending on the company who produce them. On Chart 1, RYA Training Chart 3, the land (always dry) is coloured yellow while the deepest water is white. Shallower water, from the 10m. contour to chart datum blue, potentially dry areas, chart datum to the high water limit green. The numbers in the white and blue areas of the chart are charted depths noted in

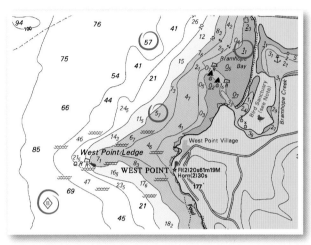

Chart 1 – For depths between soundings, some interpolation may be needed

metres and tenths of metres. Two depths, one of 57m. and another of 5.7m. have been highlighted. These depths can be considered as a minimum, there is almost always some extra depth, the height of tide, to add to those numbers. Inshore in

the green area of Bramhope Bay, we have highlighted another number, 1.1m. with a small line under it. This number shows the 'Drying Height' – the height that the sand would appear above water, if the water level was at Chart Datum.

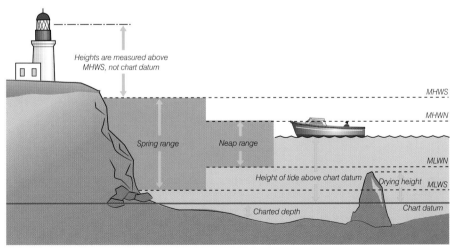

This is a cross section showing the relationship between the sea bed, chart datum, water level and the various tidal limits.

■ DEALING WITH MAGNETIC AND TRUE BEARINGS

A common source of confusion and error arises from a phenomenon known as 'magnetic variation'. The lines of longitude, as shown on the chart, are aligned in a direction leading to a fixed point at the top of the world – True North Pole. All charted information involving bearings – such as leading lines, light sectors, and tidal streams – are expressed relative to True North and, when plotting on your charts, you must do the same.

Courses and bearings should be plotted as 'true' – customarily abbreviated to 'T'. Unfortunately, hand bearing and steering compasses point towards the Magnetic North Pole, which is not only located several hundred miles from True North but drifts slowly around with time.

This error is known as Variation and is named East or West depending upon which side of True North the Magnetic Pole lies (see Fig 1). Clearly, a correction must be applied to all Magnetic bearings ('M') before they can be laid off on the chart as True.

To find out what the variation is on the large-scale charts we use in this book, the value of variation in any given area can be found on the 'compass rose' nearest to our position. In our example, we are told that variation in 2005 was 7° 25' West. The variation is changing (reducing) by 8 minutes to the east annually. So, three years later (2008) variation will have reduced by 24' – reducing it to a convenient 7°W.

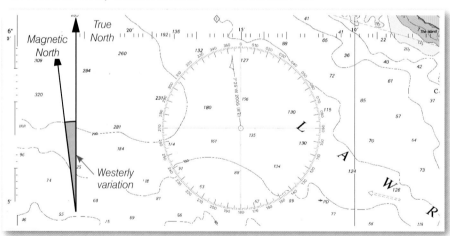

Fig 1

TIP
    An easy way to convert True into Magnetic bearings is to use the rhyme "west is best and east is least" as an aide memoire, meaning that if variation is west then the magnetic bearing will be larger than the true by the value of variation. And if variation is east then the magnetic will be less than the true bearing again by the value of variation. To convert M into T the reverse applies.

POSITION FIXING

In Fig 2 our intrepid skipper is on his way to Victoria Harbour. It's dark and about 2½ hours before HW Victoria. He is making a steady 5 knots but knows that the tidal streams are strong in this area so decides that he would like to fix his position.

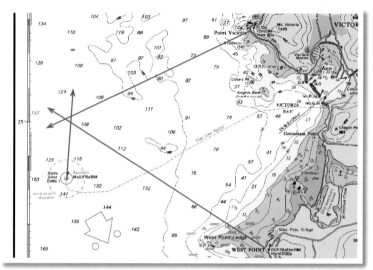

Fig 2 – Two bearings are enough to obtain a position, but three are much better

- He decides to use a 'three point fix'. Using his hand bearing compass he takes bearings on Point Victoria LH (072°M), West Point LH (129°M) and lastly the Alpha Juliet Delta 1 Platform (191°M).
- Next he converts all bearings to T and plots them on the chart. This establishes a fix some 2 miles north of the platform. Note that, due to small errors, bearings rarely cross exactly. Even the best efforts usually result in a small triangle, known down the ages as a 'cocked hat'. If you get a big cocked hat, you've probably made a mistake. Have another go.

IMPORTANT: When plotting latitude and longitude be careful to check that you are interpreting the graduations correctly.

Also understand that the lines of longitude converge towards the poles and therefore cannot be used to measure distances. However the scale of Latitude remains constant. Therefore, only the Latitude scale at the sides of the chart can be used for distance measurement.

1 minute of latitude = 1 nautical mile

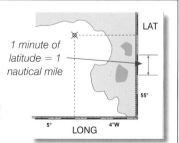

■ MAGNETIC COURSE TO STEER

With the position fixed our skipper decides to work out a Course to Steer into the southern entrance to Victoria Harbour.

1. He draws the ground track (the line that he wants to follow) from his position to the harbour entrance.
2. Next he needs to plot the tide vector. The tidal atlas (see page 52) for 2 hours before HW Victoria shows a tide stream in his locality running at 2.9 knots (it is Spring tides) in a direction of 175°T. He plots the vector on the chart from his position fix and gives the line a length of 2.9 nautical miles, which represents one hour of tide.

3. He anticipates 5 knots of boat speed so adjusts his dividers to 5 miles, places one point on the end of the tide vector and turns it till it intersects the ground track. The line drawn between these last two points is the course to steer – in this case 051°T. Applying variation gives him 58°M, which is his course to steer to counter the tidal stream. The tidal stream is likely to be weaker inshore, so the passage will take about 1 hour 30 minutes.

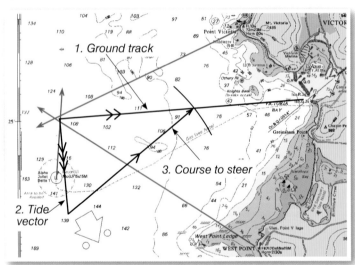

Actually an experienced navigator will anticipate a reduction in the tide stream in the last mile or so of the approach and look for a transit of some background lights above the entrance, once it is clearly identified.

NOTE: Although nautical miles were used here to complete this plot, any convenient units would have produced the same result. Many navigators prefer to use the graduations along the edges of their Breton type plotters, dispensing with their dividers altogether. Incidentally, this type of plotter can be set up to automatically compensate for variation.

■ TIDE TIMES AND HEIGHT OF TIDE

Times and heights of tides can be obtained either from local tide tables or an almanac. Shown right is an extract from the RYA Training Almanac for the port of Victoria. We are interested in the times and height of tide in the morning of 28th April and have circled the entry for that day. Appearing on the page will be a note informing us that the times given are in UT (Universal Time). Therefore we must add one hour to the times given for our particular day to account for British Summer Time.

The time of high water is 10.56 UT (11.56 BST). And the height of tide at that time will be 6.0m., the height of the previous low water was 0.3m.

If we want to know the height of tide at some time between low and high water on that morning, we can put that information onto the tidal curve for Victoria on page 36 of the Almanac, shown below.

The curve is a clever graph, linking time to height of tide. We put our BST HW time in the HW box at the foot of the curve.

26 0207 1.4 0822 5.2 TU 1438 0.9 2055 5.3	**11** 0338 1.2 0943 5.3 TH 1555 1.0 2207 5.2	**26** 0314 0.6 0927 5.£ F 1542 0.2 2155 5.7
27 0256 1.0 0908 5.6 W 1523 0.4 2138 5.6	**12** 0407 1.0 1013 5.4 F 1623 0.9 ● 2234 5.¦	**27** 0357 0.4 1011 6.0 ⊙ 1625 0.¦ O 2236 5.8
28 0339 0.6 0951 5.9 TH 1606 0.1 O 2219 5.8	**13** 0435 .9 1043 .4 SA 1650 .8 2301 .¦	**28** 0440 0.3 1056 6.0 SU 1707 0.2 2319 5.8
29 0420 0.3 1034 6.1 F 1649 0.0 2300 5.9	**14** 0504 0.9 1114 5.4 SU 1719 0.9 2330 5.3	**29** 0¦¦¦ ¦.¦ 1141 5.8 M 1751 0.5
¦0 0¦0¦ 0.2 ¦.¦	**1¦** 0535 ¦.¦ 1145 ¦.¦	**¦0** 0002 5.6 0¦0¦ ¦.¦

Next we find the HW height (6.0m.) on the top scale and the LW height (0.3m.) on the bottom scale. A line drawn between those heights then represents the range of tide for that morning.

If we want to know the Height of Tide at 2 hours before HW, we can start at that point on the time scale (09.56), follow it up to the curve, go across to the range line and then up again to the height scale, where we can read the Height at 4.77m.

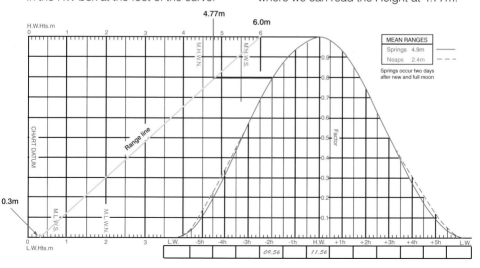

■ TIDAL ATLASES / DIAMONDS AND RATE OF FLOW

When navigating in tidal waters you will often need to know the direction and speed of the stream. You have two main sources of information: the chart, and tidal stream atlases. Atlases give the most complete picture, with a separate page for each hour of the tidal cycle and arrows showing the direction of flow. Numbers show the speed at 'spring' tides (higher numbers) or 'neaps' (lower numbers). Beware, the rates are often shown in tenths of a knot.

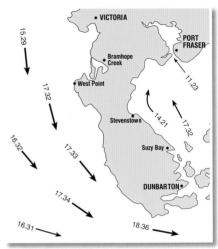

Tidal atlases give instant information on the tidal situation at any time

The extract (right) shows the situation 2 hours before HW at Victoria. The time is as we have seen in the almanac extract of HW at Victoria. So it's easy to relate the pages to real time of day.

Looking about 3 miles off West Point we can see that the stream is flowing to the SSE at 3.2 knots on Spring tides (1.7k at neaps). This information is found on the chart but in numerical format. Look back at the chart on page 47 (Victoria Harbour). Again 3 miles off West Point you will find a Tidal Diamond 'B'. The tidal data for that point can be found on a table located elsewhere on the chart.

Locate the table (see extract below) and, in this case, follow the Diamond 'B' column down to the line for 2 hours before HW, we have underlined the Direction (165°T) and the spring rate (3.2 knots) and neap rate (1.7 knots). You should interpolate between springs and neaps. You will find several other tidal diamonds scattered about the chart. Always use the one closest to your position.

Hours		Geographical Position	Directions of streams (degrees)	Rates at spring tides (knots)	Rates at neap tides (knots)		◇A 46°20'5 N 5 50·0W			◇B 46°20'6 N 6 18·4W			◇C 46°11'2 N 5 43·2W		
Before High Water	6					-6	110	1·8	0·8	158	1·0	0·6	189	1·7	0·9
	5					-5	108	1·0	0·5	153	1·7	0·8	192	1·1	0·6
	4					-4	026	0·4	0·2	159	2·8	1·5	290	0·6	0·4
	3					-3	297	1·4	0·7	154	3·9	2·0	359	1·5	0·8
	2					-2	278	2·0	1·1	165	3·2	1·7	004	1·8	0·9
	1					-1	274	1·7	0·8	173	2·4	1·3	007	1·4	0·7
High Water						0	271	1·1	0·5	186	1·2	0·7	010	0·9	0·5
After High Water	1					+1	170	0·5	0·3	349	1·1	0·6	173	1·2	0·6
	2					+2	111	1·6	0·8	341	3·0	1·6	179	1·6	0·8
	3					+3	114	1·8	0·9	338	3·7	1·8	185	1·9	1·0
	4					+4	113	2·2	1·2	342	3·9	2·0	187	2·1	1·2
	5					+5	112	2·0	1·0	341	2·8	1·5	189	2·0	1·1
	6					+6	110	1·8	0·9	355	2·3	1·2	190	1·8	0·9

■ GLOBAL POSITIONING SYSTEM (GPS) AND CHART PLOTTERS

GPS relies on a minimum of at least twenty-four satellites orbiting above the Earth's surface. Even the most basic GPS units will do far more than display latitude and longitude.

Other useful functions include:

Speed over the ground (SOG) – This can differ from speed through the water because the latter may be affected by tidal stream. SOG is the actual progress you are making.

Course over the ground (COG) – Otherwise known as the ground track. This is often different from your compass course which may be allowing for the stream. COG is the actual direction in which you're progressing.

Waypoint – Is a position you want to head towards. It may be your final destination or it could be a point where you intend to change course – such as a course alteration off a headland. Waypoints can usually be named and stored in your GPS. They can often be strung together as 'routes' and, in many cases, 'reverse routes', so you can follow the same track there and back. Many GPS sets have a 'Go To' button which will give you the course and distance to a waypoint of your choice. Then, as you head towards it, they are able to show Cross Track Error (XTE) if you stray off the ground track.

Chart plotters combine the position finding function with electronic charts, showing your position and track in relation to your surroundings.

Chart plotters come with a wealth of useful navigational tools

PART 4: BOAT HANDLING TEST FOR SAIL AND POWER

1. BEFORE SETTING OUT

- Has listened to weather forecasts.
- Give safety briefing including use of safety equipment.

- Pre-start engine checks.
- Start engine.
- Check cooling.
- Know fuel range.

PLANNING

All skippers putting to sea are required to have a passage plan. So it's sensible to expect that a Practical Assessor will want to see that a candidate for an ICC has put together the basic information for a plan for the day. Passage plans for small boats don't need to be extensive or fully written out, but a few notes in your logbook will prove that the subject has been covered.

So what are the essential bits of information?

- A current weather forecast comes first. There's no good reason for going to sea without one, when good reliable forecasts are available from so many sources. Candidates should expect to be questioned on the implications of the forecast with regard to sea state etc. in the local area.

- Tidal planning comes next. The candidate should be aware of tide times, (high and low water), tidal heights and the direction of flow and how those effects will impact on local navigation. An understanding of the direction of tidal flow will be essential, for instance, when coming alongside or picking up a buoy. Except for the weather forecast, all of the other information will be found in the current almanac.

BRIEFING

A general safety briefing at the start of a passage should be a matter of habit on any well run boat. For any manoeuvre to be successful, all members of the crew need to understand what's going on and what's expected of them. The ability to deliver a clear and succinct briefing is a good indicator of the skipper's level of crew control and assessors will want to hear one before each manoeuvre.

In a more basic sense.

- It is essential that somebody on board, other than the skipper, should know how to turn the engine on and off.

- Make an emergency call on the radio.

- Where to take the boat in the event of the skipper's loss and so on.

2. DEPARTING FROM A PONTOON

■ Understands use of springs to depart from leeward wall/pontoon.
■ Communicate with crew.
■ Position fenders correctly.

Before you depart, take a few moments to observe the direction of the stream. Tidal planning may have told you that it's ebbing at 2 knots but looking over the side may reveal that you are in fact sitting in a back eddy. Having decided whether you want to depart bow or stern first (remember the stream!) take a few more moments to single up (reduce the mooring system to the minimum number of lines) and set up the remaining lines so that they can be slipped from onboard. It's never a good idea to leave crew on the dockside.

If the wind is offshore departing is easy. Slip either the bow line or stern line shortly before the other and the boat will happily blow away from the mooring.

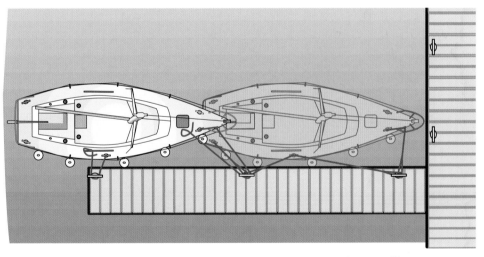

When singling up, it sometimes helps to move the boat to a better position

SPRINGING OFF

An onshore wind complicates a departure, as it tends to hold the boat against the pontoon/wall. This situation calls for a procedure known as 'springing off'. The principle works whether you are leaving bow or stern first, so let's start with going out forward.

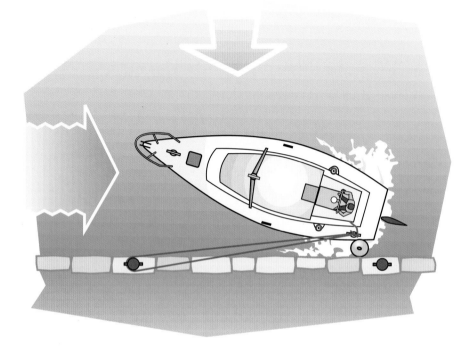

1. Rig a slipping stern spring line from the boat's stern to the pontoon and put an extra fender on the quarter next to the pontoon/wall.

2. First engage a little reverse power then slip the stern line.

3. When you are clear to leave, slip the bow line and watch the stern swing towards the pontoon/wall.

4. As the fendered quarter makes contact with the wall, increase the reverse power until the bow has pulled away from the wall far enough for the stream to act on the hull and keel to help the bow pull out further.

5. Once you are confident that you have a clear line of departure ahead, put the engine into neutral, slip the spring, engage forward gear and drive away.

The same technique can be applied when leaving stern first.

1. Rig a slipping bow spring line from the boat's bow to the pontoon cleat and return it to the bow. Put a fender as far forward as possible.

2. You can then motor gently forward, slip the bow and stern lines but hold tight on the spring. Now increase the forward thrust and steer the stern away from the pontoon.

3. When you have enough clearance select neutral, slip the spring, and when you are sure that you have a clear line of departure aft, engage reverse gear and go.

This solution can be applied even in extreme circumstances. In the next diagram it's time to leave, but we are deep in a marina with a strong wind blowing us onto our berth.

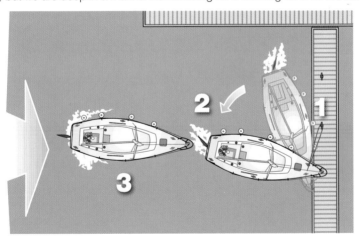

1. Again, rig a nice long slipping bow spring with plenty of fenders near to the bow.
2. Motoring forward against the spring, push the bow into contact with the pontoon and, with steadily increased revs, steer the stern up into the wind.
3. With stern dead to wind, select neutral, slip the spring and – after checking for snags – reverse away.

3. PERFORM A 360° TURN IN A CONFINED SPACE

For all helmsmen, the ability to turn a boat at almost zero speed and in little more than its own length is an absolutely vital skill. The manoeuvre should be practised before it's needed – ideally in open water where no damage will be caused should things go wrong.

Aboard a single screw yacht, we have entered a marina and drifted to a halt in the fairway, only to discover that the berth that we have been allocated is filled. There is no stream or significant wind to worry about. Here's what to do:

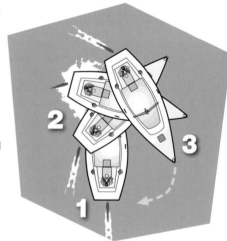

1. Give the boat full starboard helm and use a couple of short bursts of forward power to start her turning to starboard.

2. The moment you sense the boat moving forward, apply a good burst of astern power, still keeping the helm hard over to starboard. This will both kick your stern to port and pull the yacht backwards.

3. Repeat this sequence until you have turned 180° then motor smoothly out the way you came in.

Twin-screw motor yachts can achieve the same result by using forward gear on one engine and reverse on the other.

Now for a boat with a single steerable drive, drifted to a halt on the centreline of the fairway:

1. Select full starboard lock and give a couple of bursts forward. The boat's stern will kick out to port turning the boat to starboard.

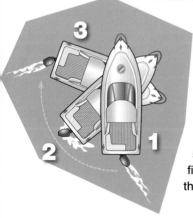

2. As soon as you sense the boat moving forward, select neutral, apply full port lock and give a couple of bursts astern. The stern will again kick to port and the boat will pull astern with the bow effectively still turning to starboard.

3. Select neutral, full lock to starboard and a couple more forward bursts should complete the 180° turn. If not, repeat the sequence. Spinning the wheel from side to side is a more energetic process than on a fixed screw vessel, and one in which observance of the 'steer before gear' rule is essential.

4. SECURING TO A BUOY

- Communicate effectively with crew.
- Prepare warp.
- Choose correct angle of approach.

- Control speed of approach.
- Secure boat effectively.
- Depart from the mooring safely.

Mooring buoys come in many shapes and sizes but those reserved for visitors will be large, clearly visible and are often marked with 'V' or some other identifying mark or colour, which may be indicated in the almanac. They may, however, have pick up buoys attached. If the mooring has a pick up buoy then approach into the stream with a crew on the foredeck armed with a boathook. Remember that the buoy will disappear under your bow as you approach so ask the crew to call out the distances while pointing at it with the hook.

Once the boat has been brought to a halt with its bow over the buoy, your crew should sweep under the pick up buoy's line with the boathook, pull it aboard – ideally over the bow roller or through a fairlead – and secure it to a cleat. You can then relax and put the kettle on.

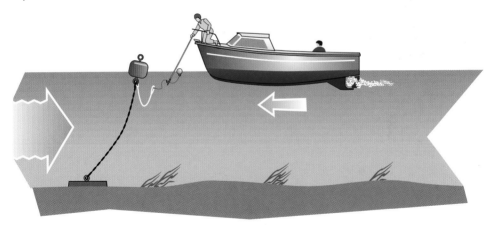

Always approach against the stream

It's a little more difficult if there isn't a pick up buoy. Even if you succeed in grabbing the ring in the top of the mooring buoy with your boathook, it's all too easy to lose the battle against the full force of wind and stream. Unfortunately, once a boathook is under load it becomes very difficult to unhook so you may be faced with the decision either to let it go or follow it overboard.

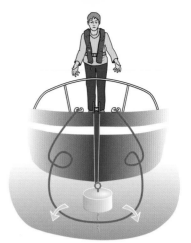

The easier method is to use a lasso. Take both ends of a long and heavy mooring warp and cleat them to the boat with 'figure of eights' – which can always be undone, even under load. Pass the large loop of rope out over your bow roller and then back aboard over the rails. The foredeck crew should now divide the loop of rope into two even handfuls and, when the helmsman brings the boat to a halt, cast the rope out and over the buoy. As the rope settles and sinks, back away from the buoy and the rope will pull tight around the chain beneath the buoy.

Lassoing a buoy is often safer than trying to hook it

Whether by lasso or boat hook, if you have to pick up a mooring single-handed, make the initial connection over the stern where you can both drive the boat and reach the buoy. Once you have your temporary connection, take a long warp from the bow to the buoy, release the stern and allow the boat to swing. Finally, pull the bow up to the buoy and secure.

> **WARNING: Never be tempted to make a loop in the end of a warp with a bowline and cast that over a buoy 'rodeo' style. You may not be able to release it later.**

MAKING FAST

Remember that a lassoed buoy is not a secure mooring – just a temporary attachment until you attach securely.

Once the initial connection is made you can pull both parts of the lasso together, bringing the boat and buoy close enough to put a proper mooring line through the ring in the top of the buoy. Boats with high freeboard may need to launch a dinghy.

When rigging a more permanent mooring line, pass it through the buoy's ring twice, making a full turn. This will allow the rope to partially grip the ring, thus reducing movement and the frictional wear that comes with it. In lively conditions, a single pass through the ring can burn through rapidly.

Where there may be lots of movement, a prudent skipper will rig a second, slack mooring line, just in case the first one fails.

Reduce wear by taking a round turn

PICKING UP BUOYS – WIND AGAINST STREAM

A strong wind blowing in the opposite direction to the stream could be one situation where it may be tempting to ignore an important principle. DON'T. Always steer into the stream.

We are motoring towards a mooring buoy facing a 2-knot tide, with a near gale blowing from astern. The wind is pushing us forward at an alarming rate. At 20 metres from the buoy we engage reverse gear to slow the boat down. At 5 metres we increase the reverse thrust so that the boat is slowed further until the bow is held stationary over the buoy. Even though we are using a lot of reverse thrust to hold the boat against the wind we still have 2 knots of positive flow over the rudder and, therefore, retain full control. It's worth noting that single screw motorboats with small rudders and big propellers may not have much control by rudder alone, though the principle holds good.

The skipper shown below is getting it wrong. He will find himself dead in the water with no control, while overshooting the buoy.

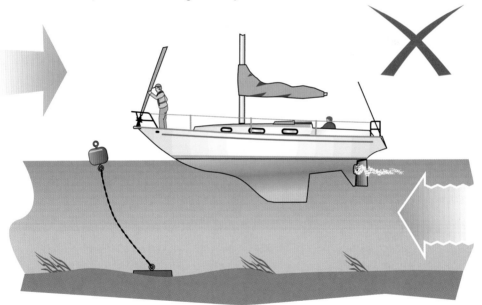

Resist the temptation to approach upwind. It's the stream you need to be concerned about

TIP If you are unsure about the direction of the tide, go and have a look at the buoy first. You will probably be able to see the stream flowing around it or perhaps a pick-up buoy resting on the down tide side.

5. MAN OVERBOARD (MOB)

■ Observe the MOB or instruct crew to do so.
■ Demonstrate correct direction
  and speed of approach.
■ Make suitable contact with MOB.

*A man overboard can be difficult to spot in rough conditions. It's
very important to try and keep him in sight at all times*

If anyone falls off of a vessel underway, it's a life-threatening situation – certainly one
that demands a Distress (Mayday) call on the VHF radio. In reasonable conditions it
might seem that the chances of recovering the casualty are very good, but things have
a tendency to go from bad to worse, in which case you will need the assistance of the
rescue services. Even if you recover the MOB, he may have been injured, might be
hypothermic or in shock – in which case a medical evacuation may be required. So
make the distress call as soon as possible.

But, the question is when? If you have crew to spare, there's no problem. Detail
one of them to make the call while you go about organising the recovery. If single
handed you will have to prioritise your actions. If you have a VHF radio with DSC facility,
consider pressing the distress button on your DSC set early. This will then send an
automatic distress signal and give the coastguard a position. You can get back to the
voice message later. Or perhaps you could use a hand held VHF while remaining in the
cockpit.

There is no standard drill for MOB recovery. For one thing, you don't know which part of your finely honed team is going to be the casualty. So you need to work out a manoeuvre that works with your boat, your gear and your likely crew. Practising your chosen manoeuvre is essential and having your crew be aware of the first reactions could mean the difference between life and death. Keep the following points in mind when deciding on the best procedure for you.

When someone goes over the side we need to get back to them as soon as possible, because in cold water their potential survival time may not be long. The following are of great importance:

■ We need to stay as close as possible to the casualty throughout the manoeuvre, so that we don't lose sight of them. If crew numbers allow, it's a good idea to detail one person to continually point to the MOB.

■ We don't want to injure the MOB in our approach, either with the prop, by running him down, or by having the boat crash down on him in heavy seas. This means we must approach him carefully and slowly.

■ Lastly, we must maintain our ability to manoeuvre.

DIFFERENT TYPES OF BOAT

The problem is that a manoeuvre that works well on one boat could be disastrous on another. For instance, a slow moving displacement motorboat might immediately put its engine controls into neutral and carry out a quick turn, while a sudden stop on a fast moving, planing boat might well lead to injuries among those still aboard. And, while a sailing cruiser with a fixed backstay can immediately turn through the wind (heave to) in order to stop close to the casualty, an old gaffer or racing yacht with running backstays might well lose their rig if they attempted the same. Before we look at some manoeuvres that do work for various boat types, it's worth noting that none of them involve approaching the casualty directly upwind.
In all cases, the first reactions should be:

■ The first person to see the emergency should shout 'MAN OVERBOARD' to alert the whole crew.

■ Someone should press the MOB button on the GPS or chart plotter.

■ Someone should point at and maintain constant visual contact with the casualty.

SAILING CRUISERS

Modern sailing cruisers have relatively small mainsails and efficient auxiliary engines. They should use their sails to stop the boat and then use their engines to manoeuvre for a pick up.

1. The casualty falls off while the boat is cruising along on a beam reach.

2. As soon as he is aware of the problem the helm turns the boat through the wind, effectively heaving to. The engine is started.

3. The mainsail is sheeted in tight to reduce any drive from it and to prevent it swinging across the cockpit. Roll or drop the jib.

4. The skipper then drives the boat to a stop upwind of the casualty and across the wind. Using reverse and forward drive as required he allows the boat to drift down onto the casualty beam on. The MOB is recovered from the leeward side.

There are several advantages to this approach. It is gentle; the boat and casualty rise and fall together with any wave action, the boat provides a lee to the MOB and the connection should be positive without any tendency for the boat to drift away. Furthermore, in strong winds the boat will be heeled towards the casualty making the pick up easier.

SAILING YACHTS WITH LARGE MAINSAILS, RUNNING BACKSTAYS, ETC.

Some yachts cannot be 'crash tacked' without risking the loss of the rig, making an already dire situation worse. Any sailboat with a powerful mainsail – one that will out-power her engines – or running backstays essential for supporting the mast falls into this category. These boats need a little bit of crew organisation before they tack, and their final approach line should be at that magical 60° to the wind angle so that the mainsails can be eased and left shaking (de-powered) through the final stages of the manoeuvre.

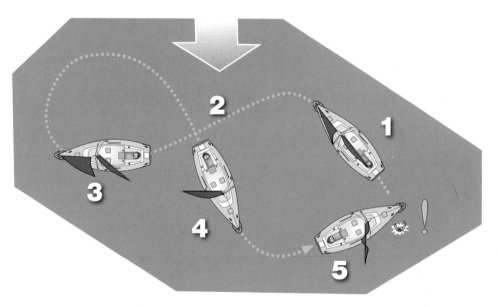

Some yachts must make a more elaborate approach

1. The casualty goes overboard with the boat close hauled.

2. The skipper bears away onto a beam reach as soon as he is aware of the MOB. He tells the crew to prepare to tack the boat, dropping the jib in the tack.

3. Once through the wind, he bears away onto a broad reach and starts the engine.

4. Easing the mainsail completely, the skipper turns his leeward bow towards the casualty.

5. With the mainsail flapping and de-powered, he can now use the engine to manoeuvre the boat to a standstill with the casualty alongside his leeward beam, ready for a pick up.

PART 4: BOAT HANDLING

LARGE MOTOR BOATS

1. At somewhere above 20 knots, a crewmember falls off the stern.

2. Having heard the Man Overboard call, the helmsman checks behind him and slows down smoothly, so as to avoid injury to those on board.

3. He then turns as fast as possible, safely, while looking back down his wake line for the casualty.

4. Steering back into his wake line, the helm assesses the wind direction and, once the MOB has been pinpointed, he manoeuvres the boat to stop upwind of the casualty and across the wind.

5. Using forward and reverse on the engine furthest from the MOB in the water, he allows the wind to push the boat sideways towards the MOB.

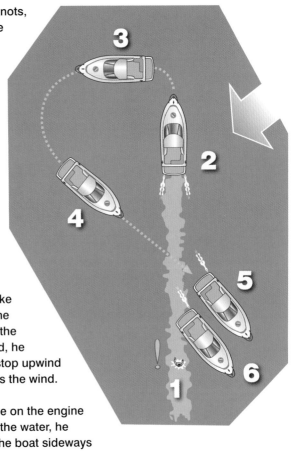

6. While his remaining crew lasso the casualty, move him back along the leeward side, and then drag him aboard the bathing platform, the skipper stays close to his controls making sure that the engines are in neutral while the MOB is close alongside.

RIBS AND SMALL POWERBOATS

The manoeuvre for RIBs and other small powerboats is very similar to the manoeuvre for large motor yachts except that the final pick up should be on the windward bow. This keeps the MOB as far away from the props as possible and eliminates the risk of a boat with such a shallow draught being blown over him. Another point to consider is the position of your engine controls. If they are on the starboard side of the boat, as in our example, then it's best to roll the casualty back on board on the port side so that the activity on deck is well away from them.

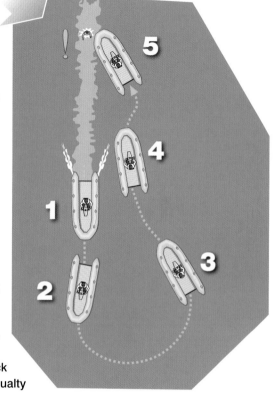

1 & 2. **The helmsman hears the Man Overboard call, slows down gradually and turns back into his wake.**

3 & 4. **Driving back along his wake line, he finds the casualty and then manoeuvres to make a pick up on his port bow with the casualty to windward.**

5. Once alongside he stops his engines before he and the rest of his crew busy themselves rolling their wet crewmate back on board.

LIFEBUOYS, DANBUOYS AND LIGHTS

In rough seas, throw the danbuoy overboard as soon as possible after the MOB has fallen, even if you believe it may be out of his reach. It will give you a point to aim for if you lose sight of the person and they may even be able to swim to it. Any lifebuoy without a danbuoy attached is probably best kept until you are within a reasonable throwing distance of the casualty, most likely as you make your approach. You may have to abort the approach and go around again.

RECOVERY METHODS

If your casualty is conscious, stop the boat a few metres away and use a buoyant throwing line to pull him towards the boat. Once alongside, secure the MOB with a loop of rope, so that he can't float away, before lifting. If the casualty is unconscious or unable to help, use a loop of rope as a lasso to pull him alongside and secure him.

Halyard

Once he's alongside, a sailboat with a large crew, or large winches, can simply use a halyard (spinnaker halyards are best) to hoist the casualty on board. Small crews, however, may want to keep a powerful 'block and tackle' handy that can be attached to a spare halyard or a boom to hoist in a heavy casualty. Traditional displacement motor boats with short masts

A proper lifting sling (left) is best but a loop of rope will do

or davits can use similar methods to hoist casualties over their rails while most modern style cruisers have a low bathing platform aft that can be used as a recovery point.

There are a number of proprietary MOB recovery devices on the market, some using buoyant strops, and some working on the parbuckle principle. They all have their pros and cons, but whatever boat type you have, work out a system for hoisting a heavy casualty back aboard that works with your gear and your crew, and then practise.

Remember, it may be you.

TREATMENT OF A COLD CASUALTY

- Change the casualty into dry clothes.
- Re-warm slowly.
- Give warm drinks.
- Use thermal protective aids such as foil blankets to retain body heat.
- Monitor and record reflexes and symptoms.
- Obtain medical assistance. If at all in doubt, have him checked over once back ashore.

6a: HIGH SPEED MANOEUVRES (POWER DRIVEN CRAFT ONLY)

- Where fitted, kill cords must be used!
- Choose suitable area.
- Show awareness of other water users.

- Warn crew before each manoeuvre.
- Look around before S and U turns.
- Control speed on U turns.

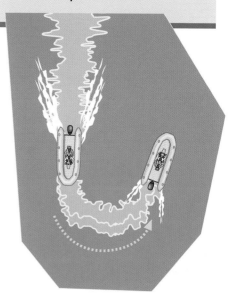

For this part of the assessment power boaters must find some open water, where they have room to manoeuvre and where neither they, nor their wash will upset other vessels or water users.

They will be asked to manoeuvre through a series of circles and 'S' bends while demonstrating both full control and correct use of trim tabs or engine leg adjustment. They should be prepared to show the assessor that they are fully aware of all other traffic by looking over both shoulders before turning (right) or slowing down. They must then be able to bring the craft back to a slow speed safely.

INCREASED SEA STATE

In an increased sea state power boaters should select an appropriate speed for the wave height and period. They might also trim the bow down (below), to avoid 'launching' off waves, or maybe steer a zig-zag course upwind to lengthen the run between wave crests (right). If running with the sea the bow should be trimmed up.

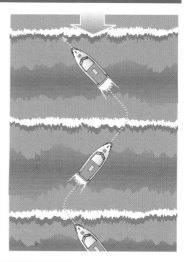

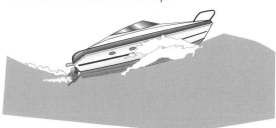

6b. HANDLING UNDER SAIL

- Sail triangular course with one leg to windward.
- Choose suitable area for hoisting/ lowering sails.
- Use sails suitable for prevailing conditions.
- Show awareness of wind direction.

- Trim sails correctly on each point of sailing.
- Warn crew before each manoeuvre.
- Look round before tacking or gybing.
- Control sails when tacking and gybing.

Skippers of sailing boats will need to demonstrate their ability to sail upwind and downwind safely and efficiently. To begin with, candidates should select a sensible place, not too exposed, free of traffic and with enough room to manoeuvre, to hoist sail. They should select a balanced sail plan suitable for the conditions remembering that they will be expected to exhibit safe, controlled, rather than fast sailing techniques.

Sail triangular course with one leg to windward.

They will need to show the assessor that they have full control when tacking or gybing. Commands when going into either manoeuvre should start with a warning to the crew, followed by a good look around to make sure that there is room to continue. A further warning should precede the movement of the helm with, if necessary, short commands to release and haul away on sheets. When gybing, booms should be 'centred' by hauling in on the mainsheet before being eased quickly on the new side. Avoid 'crash gybes'!

When beating, helms should be capable of tacking from one close-hauled line to the other without excessive 'over-steering'. They should further demonstrate good control, avoiding excessive heel, or weather helm, by easing the mainsheet or even reefing.

7. COMING ALONGSIDE A WINDWARD PONTOON

- Communicate effectively with crew.
- Show awareness of other water users.
- Prepare warps and fenders.
- Choose correct angle of approach.
- Control speed of approach.
- Stop boat in place required and secure to pontoon.
- Stop engine.

MIDSHIPS SPRING

Before looking at specific berthing strategies, it's worth describing the midships spring – an extremely useful tool, particularly when short-handed. Many finger berths are so short that bow and stern lines alone won't hold a boat in position – it takes a couple of additional spring lines to do that, and they can't be rigged in a hurry.

However, a midships spring will hold your boat alongside, totally under control, for as long as it takes to get your other mooring lines sorted. Here's how to go about it.

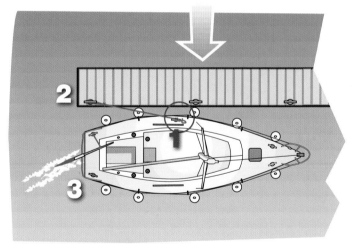

1. Secure the spring to the midships cleat (circled) and make a loop in the other end.
2. As the boat comes alongside, a crewmember steps ashore and drops the loop over a convenient cleat on the pontoon.
3. Motor gently ahead against the spring, steering the stern in against the pontoon. As long as you keep the power on, the boat will be held in place, even in a weather berth. Motor boats with their pivot points a long way aft may find that a stern line works better.

SECURING TO A WINDWARD FINGER BERTH

Going into a marina we have been allocated a windward berth, port side to. We know that as we slow the boat to pick up the mooring, the wind will push us away from the berth, so we need to be quite positive in our approach, maximising the effect of momentum. There may not be enough time for more than one person to get off of the boat before the wind blows us away, so we have decided to use the single line mid-ships spring technique shown on the previous page.

1. We approach the berth at a couple of knots, keeping the bow into the wind as far as possible.

2. Now in neutral, our speed is dropping slowly and we are steering first at the end of the finger and then running the bow down the finger's edge so that the widest part of the boat is steered alongside. As it comes within reach our crew drops the pre-made loop in the end of our single mooring line over the first cleat on the end of the finger.

3. With our midships spring attached, we motor forward until the boat is alongside, when we can complete the mooring almost at our leisure.

Remember that the single line is fixed at a point midships, opposite the pivot point so we can still steer the boat effectively while we push against the line. A motorboat's pivot point is much nearer the stern, so motorboats can use a stern line to the same effect.

Note that we've prepared fenders on our port side for this manoeuvre. This gives us an escape route. If we fail to pick up the mooring or if the wind is too strong and we don't get close enough to our berth then we can stop the boat with a good burst astern and allow the wind to push us gently down on to the leeward finger (or a neighbouring boat if there is one). This is a much safer solution than attempting to reverse out to start the manoeuvre again.

SECURING TO A WINDWARD BERTH IN A STRONG WIND AND TIDE

This example shows an elegant solution to an awkward problem. It's a technique that will get you out of trouble in quite extreme conditions. Imagine we have entered a busy harbour with both the stream and wind conspiring to keep the boat off our allocated starboard side-to berth. A traditional approach simply won't allow enough time alongside to get crew and lines ashore, because as soon as we turn the boat broadside to the wind and stream both will push us away from the pontoon.

Fortunately, there's a way round this problem.

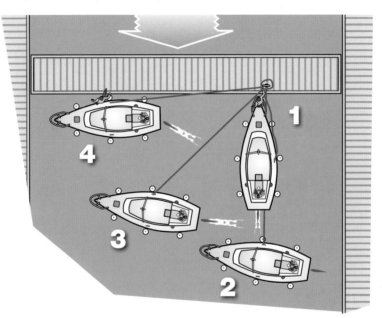

1. Motoring gently forward; carefully position the bow over the pontoon cleat that will end up just astern of the yacht when moored. Our crew has prepared a midships spring on the starboard side (see page 71) and run it forward to the starboard bow, outside all rigging, guard wires and rails. The spring has a pre-made loop in the end, which is dropped over the cleat. We now put the engine in neutral and wait for nature to take charge.

2. The boat will drop back until the spring becomes taut and will hang there, more or less broadside to the wind and stream.

3. The final part of the manoeuvre involves powering forward against the spring, steering to keep the boat parallel with the pontoon.

4. Given enough thrust, the boat will push up alongside the pontoon and we can hold it there while the crew step ashore and complete the mooring.

SECURING TO A WINDWARD BERTH IN A STRONG WIND AND TIDE

If performing this manoeuvre single-handed, make the initial approach in reverse so you will be on hand, both to drive the boat and to handle the spring over the stern.

Twin-engine vessels will certainly prefer to reverse towards a chosen stern pontoon cleat, this time dropping a prepared stern line over it. Powering forward on the outside engine will then push them onto their berth.

Single engine, steerable drive boats can also use a stern line and reverse approach or use a long, bow line and steer into it.

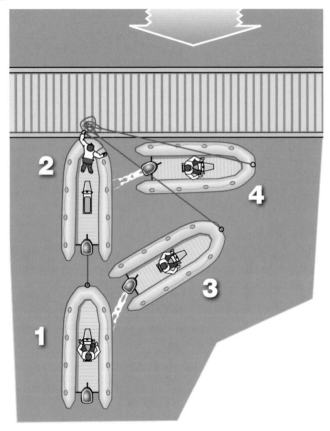

1, 2. Our RIB driver noses up to the pontoon, and drops a pre-prepared loop in the end of his painter over the cleat.

3, 4. After allowing the RIB to settle back with the wind and stream, he then applies full starboard lock and forward gear and pushes against the painter until alongside the pontoon.

ABEAM To one side of the boat.

AFT Towards the stern.

AHEAD In front of the boat.

AMIDSHIPS (MIDSHIPS) In the middle of the boat.

ASTERN Behind the boat.

BACK Sheeting a sail to windward.

BEAM The width of the boat.

BEAM REACH Sailing with the wind coming over the beam, at 90 degrees to the wind direction.

BEAR AWAY To turn away from the wind.

BEARING A direction relative to the compass.

BERTH A place to moor, or sleep.

BOLLARD A strong point to secure a mooring warp, single or double, either on the dock or the boat.

BOW The forward part of the boat. Port and Starboard bows are either side of the Stem.

BOW ROLLER A 'fairlead' for the anchor warp or tow line.

CEVNI Code Européen des Voies de la Navigation Interieure. The inland waters rules.

CLEAT A 'T' shaped strong point for securing ropes.

CLOSE HAULED Sailing to windward, as close as possible to the wind, generally steering to the sails.

CLOSE REACHING Sailing a course somewhere between a beam reach and close hauled.

COCKPIT The area below deck level but open to the weather from which a boat is controlled.

COL REGS Colloquial term for the International Regulations for the Prevention of Collision at Sea. IRPCS.

DE-POWER To spill wind from a sail and lose forward speed.

DISPLACEMENT The weight of water displaced by a floating vessel.

DISPLACEMENT MODE When a vessel is operating with its hull 'in the water' – i.e. not planing.

DOWNTIDE, DOWNSTREAM To run with the tide or stream.

DSC Digital Selective Calling. A system whereby a Radio Transmitter can make an automatic digitized call to a selected station.

FAIRLEAD A deck fitting used to lead a rope towards a winch or cleat, avoiding chafe.

FAIRWAY 'The way in', more properly that part of an approach channel lying outside a harbour entrance.

FENDERS Protective pads placed between a boat and a quay wall or pontoon.

FIN KEEL A deep, narrow, plate type keel, attached to the bottom of a boat on the centreline.

FLAGGED Carrying the flag of, and therefore registered with, a maritime nation.

FORESTAY The stay running from the bow to the mast. Fundamentally to support the mast, but also used to carry genoas and jibs.

FREEBOARD The vertical distance from the waterline to the deck.

GAFFERS Sail boats with a gaff, a spar spreading the top edge of a four cornered, fore and aft mainsail.

GENOA A foresail that overlaps the mast and mainsail.

GYBE To turn the stern of a sailing vessel through the wind.

HALYARD A rope used to hoist a sail.

HANKED ON Attached using piston hanks, or other hanks.

HEEL The amount that a boat leans over.

HELM The steering position, the tiller or wheel, non-gender specific person steering.

HELMSMAN The person steering a vessel.

IALA The International Association of Lighthouse Authorities

IRPCS See COL REGS

ISAF The International Sailing Associations Federation, the governing body for yacht racing.

JACKSTAY A wire or tape used to secure individual safety lines.

JIB Foresail that doesn't overlap the mast.

JIB SHEET Rope used to control the jib.

KICKER, **KICKING STRAP** A tackle between boom and mast used to keep the boom from lifting and to shape the mainsail. Sometimes called the VANG.

KNOT One nautical mile per hour.

LEE SHORE A shore onto which the wind is blowing.

LEECH The trailing edge of a sail.

LEEWARD The side of the boat facing away from the wind.

LEEWARD BERTH A berth that the wind pushes a boat into.

LOA Length overall.

LONG KEEL A keel that runs almost from the front to the back of a boat, along the centreline.

LUFF The leading edge of a sail.

MAINSAIL The sail attached to the back of the mast (or main mast).

MAINSHEET The rope used to control the mainsail.

MARINA A collection of berths and other facilities, provided for boaters.

MOB Man overboard.

OVERFALLS Areas of rough water associated with strong tidal streams and relatively shallow water.

PILES, PILINGS Posts driven into the sea bed for securing vessels or as navigational beacons. Also used as protection to stone or concrete walls.

PIVOT POINT The point around which a boat swivels when it is steered.

PLANING Operating a vessel fast, with the hull skidding over the surface of the water.

PONTOON A floating platform used for mooring boats.

PORT The left hand side of the boat looking forward

PORT SIDE TO Placing the port side of the vessel against the quay or pontoon.

PORT TACK Sailing with wind coming over the port side.

POWER UP Trimming the sail to provide drive and increase speed.

PREVENTER A line running forward from the boom to the deck used to prevent the boom from swinging across the deck, uncontrolled.

QUARTER The side of a vessel between Amidships and the Stern.

RAM Restricted in her Ability to Manoeuvre.

REEFING Reducing sail area as the wind rises.

RIB A rigid inflatable boat. Usually a small powerboat.

RUNNING BACKSTAYS Temporary stays used singly but as one of a pair to support the mast and provide tension in the forestay, on the windward side of the mainsail.

SAR Search and rescue.

SCREW Colloquial term for propeller.

SHEET – A rope that controls a sail.

SHEET ON To pull on a sheet, to trim it.

SHROUDS Rigging supporting the mast from the sides.

SKEG A built up section of the lower hull used to support the leading edge of a rudder.

SPADE RUDDER A rudder with no external support apart from the stock and hull bearing.

SPINNAKER POLE A spar used to support the windward clew of a spinnaker. Also commonly used to sheet the clew of a headsail to windward.

SPREADERS Struts spreading the shrouds away from the mast.

STANCHIONS Vertical rods supporting the guard rails around the deck.

STARBOARD The right hand side of a boat looking forward.

STARBOARD TACK Sailing with the wind coming over the starboard side.

STEERAGE WAY The minimum speed required to maintain control of a boat via the rudder.

STERN The back end of a boat.

STREAM The flow or movement of water, whether caused by current or tide.

TACK To sail the boat's bow through the wind. The forward bottom corner of a sail.

TIDE WAY Channels where the effect of tidal stream can be felt.

TILLER A steering bar connected to the rudder.

TRANSIT Bringing two distant objects into alignment to produce a constant line of approach.

TRANSOM A flat section of hull across the stern of a boat.

UPTIDE Upstream, running against the flow of water.

VANG See KICKER.

VARIATION The difference between True and Magnetic North.

VECTOR A force with direction.

WAKE The trail of disturbed water left behind a moving boat.

WARP A rope used for mooring or anchoring.

WINDAGE The amount by which a vessel is affected by wind.

WINDWARD (WEATHER) The side that the wind is coming from.

WINDWARD (WEATHER) BERTH A berth that a boat is blown away from.

INDEX